THE DAY
BEFORE I
DIED

JF WHITAKER

PAGE PUBLISHING, INC.
Conneaut Lake, PA

First originally published by Page Publishing 2019

ISBN 978-1-64544-913-3 (pbk)
ISBN 978-1-64701-158-1 (hc)
ISBN 978-1-64544-914-0 (digital)

Printed in the United States of America

CONTENTS

For Those Who Survived

You didn't let the moments and seconds of pain, abuse, or bullying take you out. You didn't choose a permanent solution to a temporary problem.

You recognized that resenting the abusers and bullies gives them what they want—power, your power. They are the victims. Their lives are so small they must steal power, joy, and beauty from others. Report them as the thieves they are and move on.

You did not allow yourself to be defined by the moments and seconds of sadness, hurt, and loneliness. You were not defined by the worst thing that's ever happened to you.

Focusing on problems magnifies them. When focused on problems, we shrink our lives to be safe and free of fear. Our lives then become so small we think we have nothing to lose. Living in the prisons we create limits the possibility of finding a solution.

Know there is a solution.

We did not become the victim of our stories. Our stories are just that...stories. These are experiences that happen to us on our journey to our own unique reality. These experiences are the foundations of our strength and wisdom, and they make us who we become.

A life is lost in the United States to suicide every forty seconds.

Twenty servicemen and women commit suicide every day.[1]
The second leading cause of death for teens and young adults between the ages of fifteen to twenty-four is suicide.[2]

---

[1] VA National Suicide Data Report (2005–2016) Office of Mental Health and SuicidePrevention, September 2018.

[2] National Vital Statistics System, National Center for Health Statistics, CDC.

PROLOGUE

Life became small, very small
Shrinking slowly from forever to this
day, this moment, this second
Defined by the moments and seconds of life
We are lost and found in those moments

Defined by the worst that's ever happened
Shrinking from bright and shiny to dim and dark
Living in fear and sleeping with death
Not much to lose

The quiet solution arrives
Unbidden on translucent wings
Not a cry for help or a threat
A simple step to brightness and forever

PART ONE

The Day Before They Died

Man is not the creature of circumstances;
circumstances are the creatures of man.
                                        —Benjamin Disraeli

Chapter One

THE END

The end began when the rocket attack started—heralded by noise, by darkness, and by the seconds ticking slowly.

Arriving in Vietnam in January 1969, I was just in time for the second Tet Offensive, one of the largest military campaigns of the Vietnam War. The offensives were called Tet in honor of the Vietnamese New Year, which was the day these attacks were launched. My first duty was not airborne. It was on the ground as the watch officer for the navy detachment stationed at Da Nang RVN Air Base.

As a newbie, I had night duty 6:00 p.m. to 6:00 a.m. I was surrounded by brown—brown dirt, brown buildings, and humid brown air that coated my mouth as I traveled from place to place. I walked across the base and in the quiet and still early evening even the silence was brown.

My destination, the Quonset hut we called headquarters to get briefed by the lieutenant junior grade (JG) going off duty. The long low brown outline of the Quonset hut looked like half of a drainage pipe sitting on a cement slab, flat end on the ground and then rounded on the top. These huts could house a plane or offices. The creaking of rusted metal scraping on metal broke the eerie silence as I opened the door. My first look embraced a long tiled hallway reminiscent of a shotgun house. The pattern in the tile, the color of weak pea soup, haloed by an off-white background and bright lights, welcomed me as warmly as an operating room.

The interior fluorescent lights bleached out the already unattractive pea green tiles and cast shadows in every direction. There were small offices on each side of the hallway, each only large enough for the standard government-issue gunmetal-gray desk, a file cabinet, and two gray chairs with green padded seats.

I was there to relieve Carter, who had the day shift. He was a handsome big blond Texan with a friendly slow Southern drawl. Carter, built like an ox, moved with a calculated and easy pace that exuded confidence and know-how. I'm sure no one back home messed with him. He showed me what I needed to do and what I shouldn't do. I fought to memorize every detail, thinking there was security and safety in the knowing. Night was arriving fast, too fast, and so was my fear. No way was I going to say that in my outside voice.

I kept asking Carter questions, stupid and unnecessary questions. He walked to the door, trying to wrench free of my persistent uncertainty. I swallowed hard, forcing the anxiety down deep into my gut, making sure he didn't see it.

Carter had his hand on the partially opened door when the first rocket hit close to the hut. The sound was deafening. The door, slammed shut by the concussion, hit Carter in the back, knocking the wind out of him. I heard the wind leave his lungs and wondered if it was just air or life itself. He flew headlong into the hut, his body hitting mine like a boulder hurling down a mountainside. The fluorescents went dark, leaving the only light reflecting from the stars behind my closed eyes.

We rolled ass over teakettle down the hall. We lay in silence. I could feel the fear coursing through my bloodstream, taking full possession of my body as it had already taken over my mind—more than a feeling. The fearful quiet following the first barrage was suffocating and all-consuming. It was physical, tangible, and it sucked the breath right out of me. Maybe even my life too.

Welcome to Vietnam

I lay in the silent darkness. All brown was now black. I had no comprehension of what to do or what might happen.

Carter's voice came from somewhere in the darkness. "You okay?"

I breathed; I think. He was alive. I told him I was fine. He wasn't asking about my mental condition. The emergency lights came on, casting an eerie glow from the door of each office and creating a surreal pattern on the building's interior. The pea green tiles, with my face pressed against them, made me want to puke. Seconds seemed like hours until Carter urgently ordered me to take cover. I saw the outline of his bulk scramble into the nearest office and drop under a desk. I crawled into another nearby office as a loud whistling sound egged me on.

The second rocket hit, closer this time. Then the third hit, and it seemed farther away. But was it? I tried to breathe through the black, but the air felt thick and choking, not comforting.

Carter yelled, "Okay, let's go!"

Grabbing a searchlight, he bolted from the door with me on his tail. I didn't care what might greet me out there in the darkness. *I'm not staying in this building alone.* We hit the night air just in time to see the fourth rocket hit on the road between us and the tarmac where our planes were chocked and locked for the night. We leaped into a ditch, and Carter said, "Watch."

When the next rocket exploded, the pattern became clear. This wasn't random. Someone was visually guiding the rockets toward the runway. They were not guided by electronics but by humans. My brain struggled to wrap itself around that reality.

Carter turned around and said, "There."

He pointed to a brownfield behind us where we could see the spotter. A Viet Cong had dug a tunnel into the air base. When a rocket hit, his brown head popped out of the brown earth. He assessed where the rocket landed and gave the rock-eteer the necessary course corrections toward the target, our planes. They were trying to damage or destroy our planes.

The next rocket hit closer to the runway—too close. Carter radioed a Marine standing guard in a nearby tower and alerted him to the intruder. When the last rocket lit up the horizon, the head popped up, and Carter lit up the intruder with the high-intensity beam of his flashlight.

The Marine took him out. The rocket attack ended. The silence felt loud. Carter walked off like it was all in a day's work.

Welcome to a New Reality

Left in the Quonset hut alone, with the lights restored and some measure of quiet, I wondered about my new job. I didn't want to face the darkness of midnight or what the bright light of my tomorrows might hold. I just wanted to go back home, back to the green fields of Pennsylvania, to the jobs I had before. I just wanted to be safe.

I thought of green grass, green cornstalks, green apple trees lush with new growth, and the green vines of the tomato plants lying flat on the ground, unable to stand under the weight of their fruit. I remembered running through the cornstalks hiding from my brothers, and I heard the laughs and giggles.

Not the Bedlam of a Rocket Attack

We lived on twelve acres in the farming community of Harleysville, Pennsylvania. We leased out ten of those acres to a Mennonite farmer, who lived a few miles down the road. The farmer and his family planted the field and harvested different crops throughout the year. Some of the crops were boring, but the corn that grew above our heads was an exciting playground for the daring cadre of six brothers. On the backside of the leased acreage was a dark-green forest with unknown inhabitants. It was just a copse of trees with squirrels and rabbits, but when my imagination took hold, it came up just shy of Sherwood Forest or another planet inhabited by aliens.

We weren't supposed to play in the field of corn, but who could resist? We weren't supposed to go off and try to adventure our way around the ten-acre plot, but again, who could resist? It never failed that when, on my own, I dared to brave the trek around those ten acres of corn and needle my way between the woods and the stalks, Mom would call out. It was lunchtime, dinnertime, or time to do the chores, whatever. The first refrain was a melodic "Joey!" The second call was slightly louder, but I was still Joey. After a few Joeys received no response, things changed. I went from Joey to Joseph, to Joseph Whitaker, then to Joseph Francis Matthew Whitaker inside ten minutes. I'm glad the Catholic religion allowed only one confirmation name or Matthew might have been the first of many more names strung behind. The last Joseph Francis Matthew Whitaker was usually followed by "get in this house this instant, and I mean now." The demons in the woods paled in comparison to what waited when I would eventually get back home.

We cultivated a part of the remaining two acres with a family garden that produced tomatoes, cucumbers, pumpkins, and a few other assorted vegetables. The remainder of the two acres was dotted with apple trees, a sandbox, a picnic table, an old rusted well, one big red barn, and a not-so-big faded red toolshed.

The two-story brick house used to be an inn. Rumors were that George Washington slept there on his way to Valley Forge. I'd close my eyes at night and visualize him walking up the steps of the front porch with his hand tucked in his jacket over his navel, demanding a room and breakfast.

An American Hero: I Wanted to Be the Hero

George Washington's army was probably only a few recruits more than our brood. We were a family of seven boys, three girls, Mom and Dad, one dog, and the unknown inhabitants of the woods. We needed a house the size of an inn. The house was so old there were still holes in the floor where the stovepipes once tunneled through to provide heat to the upper rooms. Someone had nailed silver pie tins over the holes. I wasn't sure if that was for privacy or to make sure one of us didn't fall through.

A huge living room ran along the entire west side of the house. When storms knocked out the power, we all used to huddle in that knotty pine-paneled living room close to the mammoth brick fireplace to keep warm.

One white winter night, when a blinding blizzard knocked the power out, froze the well, and created howling, chilling noises throughout the house, we kept a fire blazing in the fireplace for hours on end. We all wrapped ourselves in blankets and hunkered down in the living room to stay warm. I also kept alert to make sure the noises we heard were the storm and not the unknowns from the forest slipping unseen into the house.

Unfortunately, what eventually filled the house was smoke. We could not locate the source of the fire, but the smoke got very gray and very thick. We couldn't breathe, so Dad gave the evacuation order. We were in the middle of nowhere with who knows what awaiting us in the storm. The roads were closed, snow was piled higher than most of us were tall, and we were going where? What would George do?

We bundled up in winter gear and began the trek across the street to the only house nearby. Mom and the ten children, older ones carrying the younger, trudged through waist-high snow. Some of the younger sibs were crying at having been woken in the middle of the night and dragged into the cold. Dad initially remained at the burning house to await the firefighters.

The house we approached in the billowing snow and darkness of night was big and old like ours. Its looming outline reminded me of a house of horror. It was owned by a Mennonite family that we didn't know at all. They were a quiet bunch who kept to themselves and lived a silent, somewhat isolated life. We emerged from the snowdrifts and ascended the porch of the dark quiet home.

In the lead, carrying one of the younger sibs, I began banging on the front door, yelling, "Fire! Fire! Can you help us?" I was putting on my fake calm, heroic demeanor, which when articulated was just shy of a shrill panic. Unfortunately, the "can you help us?" part must have been lost in the wind or lost when my voice cracked. The neighbors opened their front door in a state of panic, thinking their house was on fire. I thought the opaque decorative glass inserts in the door were history when the door slammed against the interior wall. Stopping the family just short of leaping into the drifts, I assured them it was our house on fire and not theirs.

They trundled us all into their warm musty living room, decorated in a dusty vintage Victorian style. Old worn area carpets looked handwoven and lay spread on the floor—straight-backed chairs padded with maroon cushions with beige needlepoint were haphazardly arranged around the room. Portraits hung on the walls that reminded me of the *Addams Family* on TV. Worn hardwood floors with their own unique and silent history resonated with each footfall. The house smelled of yesterday, and there was a deafening silence that made me consider heading back out into the storm. I could hear my footsteps echo throughout the house as if it were empty. Yet despite the hour and the forbidding decor, we were welcomed and treated with kindness and generosity you would only expect from family and not strangers.

Hours later, the fire trucks arrived. They had to battle snowdrifts and closed roads to get to us. They discovered our house had wooden beams, and the extended fire in the fireplace had caused those beams to smolder and ultimately catch fire. To get water on the smoldering beams, the firefighters had to take an ax to the knotty pine paneling. The damage was extensive, and the beautiful inn lost some of its charm.

We returned to the house as the sun rose, the smoke cleared, and the smell abated. Repairs were made, but it wasn't the same old house. It still accommodated all of us, and the family returned to its daily routines and some semblance of normalcy. The routines had grown geometrically with each addition to the family.

Raising a family of ten was a daunting task, so Mom sought help. Mrs. Derstine lived nearby, and she came in once a week to help Mom with the cooking, some cleaning, and some babysitting for the brood. She drove an unadorned black car, just black on black with no chrome. Many people from this region, mostly Mennonites, would have black-on-black cars. They did not believe in flash or bling. We'd race to meet her, knowing what was in store for us in a matter of hours. We, kids, didn't care about anything except the cooking, Pennsylvania Dutch cooking at its finest. She would make chocolate chip cookies by the dozen, cakes, and pies, pies, pies. Apple coffee cake, apple strudel, and apple pies, some made from red apples and some from green. All her creations were made from scratch and the apples that grew on our trees.

Mrs. D would tell me to climb the trees and gently shake the limbs to get the apples to fall, and she would collect them in her apron. I shook the limbs, and she would say, "Okay, now stop while I pick these up, and then you can give it a good shake again." She didn't want the apples to bounce off each other and bruise. I'd wait until she was right underneath me and then shake the tree like mad, watching the apples fall on or near her. She would scramble away on her thick, stout legs and threaten me with not being allowed in the kitchen to help her cook. That was serious punishment. I can smell the bakery-like aroma wafting from the kitchen to this day. The melting hot chocolate, simmering apples, stewing tomatoes, and much, much more created an image of heaven.

That was then. I was not in the apple grove or the Pennsylvania Dutch kitchen now. I was in the bunk in a strange brown land trying to rest. Another rocket attack wrenched me from my shallow sleep. The attack aimed at the ammo dump was right on target. The heavens roared, and searing yellow flames shot skyward. The usual controlled bedlam ensued as men raced to the cocoon we called a bunker.

My planned route to safety was through the latrine, streaking between the sinks on my right and the showers on my left. I was preprogrammed to make the first right turn after I passed the sinks, skirt the outer perimeter of the toilets, and shoot through a rickety wooden door to the bunker. Calling that wooden door rickety was being kind. It had been kicked, ripped off its hinges, and slammed open against the adjacent wall so many times we were lucky to have a door at all.

The bunker was a low fortified shelter that looked like a mini-Quonset hut designed to withstand a minor hit from enemy fire and to protect us from flying debris and shrapnel. The door, low to the ground, led to a sharp, ninety-degree turn to the left immediately upon entering the bunker to ensure nothing randomly blown up by a rocket flew into the cavernous space in which we all huddled.

During these flights to safety in the middle of the night, we were usually attired in only a green helmet and skivvies—a.k.a. tighty-whities. I raced into the sink area to find a senior officer hiding under one of the sinks. He was similarly attired but brandished the fat, unlit cigar that was his trademark. He said, "Good luck out there." I paused for a second, trying to decide if I should continue my trajectory to the bunker or join him under an adjoining sink.

My decision was made by a rocket that hit far too close for comfort. The building shook, the sinks rocked, toilet water sloshed from side to side in the bowls, and the yelling outside increased. I continued my path to safety and raced out the door toward the bunker. As I flung open the door, I realized I had made the wrong choice. The entire panorama to my left was nothing but fire. It looked like the world was in flames. The ammo dump was now a cacophony of deafening and terrifying explosions with flames that appeared to reach the stars.

About to duck and enter the bunker, I saw a body in front of me. A teammate had forgotten the door to the bunker was extremely low, and at fear's full speed, he smacked his forehead on the wood beam at the top of the entryway. I couldn't determine his condition, just that he was in danger's way and blocking the entrance for those who chose to make it to the bunker rather than stay in the latrine. He hadn't donned his helmet, and his face was bloodied and unrecognizable. Reluctantly, I grabbed his bare ankles and dragged him into the bunker. I hesitated for a second because he was dressed only in his underwear, and I had to drag him across dirt and rocks to get to safety.

Now the brown dirt of Vietnam was once again streaked with red. I made the ninety-degree turn into the bunker with the soldier's feet nestled in the crook of my arms, and his body following on the ground behind me like a travois. Others immediately jumped to help ease him to safety. He remained unconscious throughout the attack. Afterward, he was transported to sick bay and never seen again. Rumor had it that he didn't make it.

* * *

In a similar attack a few days later, rockets began hammering the base, and as the alert sirens screeched, we once again streaked to the bunker. These events occurred one out of every two to three nights during the Tet holiday season and then not quite as frequently at other times. It didn't matter how many times this happened; it was unnerving to be awakened from a fitful sleep and dragged into the arms of danger. When you slept with death night after night, danger was the substance of your dreams, and fear was your bunkmate.

The two-story wooden barracks shook and threatened to topple off its foundation. We raced out, and the crew member in front of me, apparently, forgot we were on the second story of the building. The stairway hung on the outside of the building. The exit strategy from the second story was down the hall, out the door, right turn, down the steps, then a short dash to safety. The unfortunate and probably sleepy crew member raced down the hall, out the door, but did not turn right and crashed through the railing, falling headfirst onto the cement foundation of the stairwell, breaking his neck.

Panic set in even before he was awake, and it cost him his life. Perhaps it's not just enemy fire we have to fear. President Franklin Roosevelt, in his first inaugural address, said, "The only thing we have to fear is fear itself." Is that what he meant?

That it's our reactions and responses to fear? In any case, dead is still dead.

It was the Tet offensive of 1969 and North Vietnamese forces in January and February of that year launched major attacks centered on military targets near Saigon and Da Nang. The initial attacks stunned both the United States and South Vietnamese troops. Our bases were breached, but the enemy was eventually driven back. There were "mini" offensives in May and August, but none rivaled the holiday assaults.

The original Tet offensive was a campaign of surprise attacks in January 1968, and this similar offensive was launched in 1969. The Communists forces launched small waves of attacks in the late-night hours against military targets. When the sun rose the next day, the main Communist operation began, and the offensive was countrywide. More than eighty thousand Communist troops struck more than one hundred towns and cities. These offensives were the largest military operations of the Vietnam War.

The Communist forces executed thousands of people in Hue and temporarily took control of several cities. The United States and the South Vietnamese Army prevailed, but the fighting went on for several months, and the losses were catastrophic for both sides. The Communist regime lost the offensive, but the magnitude, the surprise, the "at will" nature of these attacks, and the casualties rocked public opinion in the United States. Up to this point, popular opinion was that the Communists were being defeated and incapable of launching such a massive military operation. An already unpopular war lost more public support, and the United States began negotiations to end the war, though not soon enough.

Welcome to Mortality

I wanted to go back to one of the jobs I had at home and trade it for this one where people ended up dead. In the course of "normal" employment, people sometimes receive minor injuries because "you know what" happens, but they rarely end up dead.

Harleysville, Pennsylvania, didn't offer much as a home-town—maybe three or four traffic lights, a small local grocery store, and an elementary school. The buildings lining the main street doubled as office fronts and homes to insurance agents, tax accountants, and doctors. The houses were either brick or white wood, two stories, with basements and attics. The yards were large and tree covered, which made the town tranquil and picturesque. The older I got, tranquil transformed into boring and restrictive. But it was a quiet and safe place to grow up. We ran free, walked, or rode our bikes the few miles into town to the grocery store and feared nothing.

Harleysville was also home to a renowned pill-packing plant located two blocks off the main drag. During the summers, I worked as a basic pill packer and gofer for the ladies on the second floor who sat for eight or more hours at a round conveyor belt that moved vials to be filled around and around and around. I still don't like carousels. Sometimes I would sit with them, and sometimes I took the role of warehouseman with my older brother, Billy. We moved boxes of pills from storage on the lower level to the upper level, so the ladies were never without product.

One day, Billy stationed himself on the lower level while I stood up on level 2. We were moving boxes via a conveyor belt from level 1, through a hole cut in the floor, to the upper level. Billy, horsing around, rapidly piled the boxes on the belt. He was trying his hardest to overwhelm me on the upper level. The boxes jammed in the hole in the floor, but the belt kept moving, eroding their bottoms. I imagined the boxes bursting open, raining thousands of pills down on Billy.

The ladies were on the far end of the second floor, so the conveyor system did not stop when it reached level 2. A second conveyor ran horizontally the length of the building. It was designed this way, so we didn't have to carry the boxes far. The transition from the vertical ascending conveyor to the horizontal conveyor was a square metal section of steel with rollers. My job was to receive the boxes as they emerged from the hole in the floor, push them over the wheeled section of this contraption to conveyor number two, and send them on their way. Nothing was automatic. I had to keep my eyes on conveyor number two. When the boxes neared the end of the warehouse, I would race to the end of the belt, off-load the boxes, then race back and signal for Billy to continue.

When the logjam occurred, I stepped forward with one foot on the steep and ascending vertical belt and reached down into the hole to separate the jammed boxes. Working feverishly to free the boxes, I was unaware that my left foot, the one on the conveyor, was moving up toward the stationary metal section with rollers. Freeing the last box, I straightened up, dusted off my hands, thrust out my chest, and grinned in modest self-praise. I looked down just in time to see my foot being eaten by the steel trap between the belts. I was off-balance, and I could not right myself. I stood and swayed, struggling to grasp a beam or anything to give me leverage to stand, but I couldn't find purchase. As my foot disappeared between the belt and the wheels, I let loose a scream that could have shattered glass.

Luckily, there was flooring just under the spot where my foot got trapped. I stood there wobbling, watching the belt take the skin off one side of my ankle while the rollers turned the other side black and blue. I was unable to move.

Already embarrassed by the initial bloodcurdling scream, I gently told Billy to turn off the belt. Calm under fire. Gently didn't work because there was a transistor radio blaring. Billy thought I was still horsing around with him. The boxes kept coming, so I let loose with scream number 2 at an operatic range. I was bleeding, in pain, stuck, and thinking the worst. My female coworkers heard my screams and raced to my rescue.

Now these ladies were sitting, snacking, and packing for eight or more hours a day. They were not small women. The dearest and largest of them arrived at the scene first. How she moved from the far end of the building to me at breakneck speed remains one of life's greatest mysteries. She jumped on the end of the conveyor belt and consoled me by grabbing my neck and shoulders and crushing my face into her huge breasts. Her weight on the conveyor belt crushed my foot against the floor, narrowing the gap between the belt and the wheels. This well-intended consoling caused the loss of more skin and blood. I screamed frantically, but my shrieks were muffled by her boobs. The woman was much stronger than me, and I couldn't free myself. I spasmodically waved my arms, pointing at the floor, at my foot, at the blood, and at her huge arms around my face. She finally released my head from its prison of flesh, and I was able to tell her gently to get off the fucking belt.

She stepped down, and the pain lessened. Billy finally understood that the words embedded in my screams demanded that he turn off the conveyor. He complied. Calm began to reign. The crowd grew. The owners showed up. Every worker in the plant was gawking at the kid stuck in the conveyor, but no one knew how to disassemble the wheeled section from the belt to allow my escape.

Finally, the lead maintenance man arrived, muttering his opinion of any stupid kid who would put his foot on the belt. He rummaged through his toolbox and selected what he thought was the proper tool. Pleased with his selection, he reached down to begin the intricate and ever so difficult task of extricating me from my trap, only to realize the metal section was not affixed to anything but was a separate piece just sitting on the floor between the two belts. He simply lifted that section up and out, and I was freed.

My injuries were minor, but I milked them for all they were worth, trying desperately to stay out of cleavage bondage and yet enjoy the attention.

Welcome to Bondage!

Pill packing was not my first job. I had a paper route around ten years of age. I babysat for the neighbors and friends of my parents. I mowed lawns, did odd jobs, and then became a caddy at the private golf club where my parents were members. I carried two huge bags with twelve or thirteen clubs each, weighing as much as me around a golf course for four to five hours every Saturday and Sunday for about five bucks.

My most colorful language development was honed on the golf course.

This old dude, named Perkins, refused to hire a caddy. He would rent a cart just for himself and his libations. The three other guys in his group hired caddies because they were cheaper than a cart. One caddy would carry two bags, and the other would carry only one. We often fought about whose turn it was to carry two because you made more money that way.

Perkins sped ahead in his cart with his nose in the air, his attitude thicker than the morning fog, and yelled at us to hurry and catch up. I was five feet nothing, my poundage belied the nothing part, and I was constantly resentful at Perkins: pissed is what he would've said. He always carried at least one six-pack and a flask with him every outing. By hole number 10, after the refill between nines, he felt no pain. On this outing, he was cruising down the tenth fairway, which sloped gently toward a small creek that dissected the fairway, when the god of payback struck.

Perkins had hit his drive into the creek, and he couldn't stand to lose a golf ball, so he would look for it forever. As he drove the cart, Perkins had difficulty on the downhill slope and began to lose control. He fumbled with the pedals but couldn't engage the brake and slow the cart. It picked up more speed, swerved left and right, headed unimpeded toward the creek. Perkins yelled profanities, at the top of his lungs, as the cart careened over the lip of the creek and crashed nose-first into the muddy water.

Perkins could have passed for Santa Claus if he was wearing a red jacket. The golf cart didn't have seat belts. So upon impact, Perkins lunged forward, wrapped his ample self around the steering wheel, knocked the wind out of his sails, and gently slipped over the left side of the steering wheel into the mud.

I learned some colorful words that day. More importantly, I learned sometimes it is better not to laugh so hard when you think people get what they deserve. I wet my pants laughing at old Perkins. He finished the back nine wet and muddy, and I finished right along beside him—also wet but not muddy.

I was supposedly working to fund my college education. I gave 100 percent of my earnings to Dad to "put away" for my future learning. I learned quickly that my college fund was the only thing that saved us when bad times came.

Family money problems and the resultant desperation wasn't unusual. We often went through periods of financial crisis because Dad was always gambling on the next big deal. He was going to net a fortune from golf balls in vending machines, importing or exporting stuff, or golf balls that floated on the pond's surface when your shot fell short. The floating golf balls were not a hit. They only made the situation worse. The owner of the wayward ball could see it floating on the surface of the pond usually just out of reach. If it had sunk, the owner wouldn't be so frustrated. Like the floating golf balls, all these ventures frustrated us because they couldn't be reached.

We had to do our part. Billy and I were out on a street corner selling newspapers. We yelled something like "Get your *Daily News* here!" We sold a paltry amount of newspapers. I, the very model for Rodin's Thinker, decided that if we were up on the freeway, we could sell more newspapers because there were more cars. Billy wisely opted out as I headed up to the freeway to prove my theory.

Dad came by the street corner some hours later to collect the cash and saw Billy alone. When asked about my where-abouts, Billy told the truth. Dad and Billy raced to the side of the freeway and found me on the median clutching a pile of newspapers, yelling, "Get your *Daily News* here!" as cars sped by on each side of me at fifty-plus miles per hour. I waved at my admiring audience, desperately trying to maintain control of the papers. The speeding cars created an almost unmanageable, turbulent wind effect.

Dad, desperate for me not to get killed, lifted his hands above his head like the pope offering a blessing to indicate I should stay right there. When traffic cleared, he raced to the median and snatched me up. I lost my grip on the papers, and my inventory swirled around the freeway like large snowflakes. Horns honked, and Dad huffed and puffed as he dragged me to safety. It wasn't really safety because like old Perkins, Dad was pissed. He engaged in a twenty-minute diatribe about how stupid I was and how I had put myself in harm's way. Then he asked how many newspapers I sold. Humiliating myself more, I told him none.

"Do you think people are going to stop on a congested freeway, fish in their pocket for twenty-five cents, and give it to a stupid kid for a newspaper?" he said furiously. I had to reconsider my sales model.

In return for diligently turning in my earnings for college savings, I was given a paltry weekly allowance to live on. Even when I got to college, my weekly allowance was only five dollars per week.

At the end of the fall term, I called Dad to tell him tuition was due for the next quarter. "How much time do we have?" he asked. When I told him two weeks, all I heard was angry silence.

Finally, he said, "You'll have to take out a loan. We are low on funds." Translated, that meant we were out of money; he'd spent my college fund. I had mastered the language.

I asked him why things were so difficult. I'd been working for five or six years, and I should have had enough money to make it through at least two quarters. He never really answered. I knew what had happened. The next "big deal" had just hit the skids. Once I realized this, I disconnected my hitch from the family wagon and stopped dragging that empty cart. A long-range plan for my college tuition never existed.

I took out a loan and paid the tuition. I earned my own way, working part time at numerous jobs and struggled to complete my assignments. Savings or not, I was determined to earn that degree. The stress and time involved left me with little time to socialize. I felt isolation and loneliness creeping up on me. It wasn't easy—drinking, working, and studying.

One of my jobs in college was in a doughnut shop working from 11:00 p.m. to 5:00 a.m. Early in the shift, I'd be the janitor cleaning the place up. Toward the end of the shift, I would bake and fill doughnuts. When the warm, soft dough came out of the oven, I impaled the unsuspecting delicacy on a metal rod attached to a plunger. I gently pushed down on the handle of the plunger and filled the baked goods with jelly, various crèmes, and sometimes chocolate. The stingy boss demanded just one plunge of the infusing machine. However, I filled the dough to capacity, and my doughnuts weighed about three pounds each. They were a hit on campus, and students flocked to buy them when the shop opened at 6:00 a.m. I took a dozen or two back to my dorm, and my arrival was one of the most anticipated morning events.

The tight boss thought it was time to teach me a lesson on profit and loss by calculating the difference between the cost of goods and the selling price. I, on the other hand, was calculating the rise in my popularity and thought it outweighed his silly argument. Ultimately, I was fired. He just couldn't afford to keep me on. I think jelly prices were on the rise in 1964.

I was subsequently employed as an attendant at a gas station and do-it-yourself car wash off campus. The cold water and the harsh soap prompted the college students, cranky customers, to expect me to do everything for them. Hello! What does do-it-yourself mean? The job did not measure up to my expectations and station in life, so I moved on to parking cars at the Jack Tar Hotel in Lansing, Michigan. Located right in front of the state capitol. Handsome and sophisticated in my valet uniform, I raced to the arriving guests, gave them a ticket stub, retrieved keys from them, and moved the vehicle down the steep and curvy lane for safe parking in the underground garage. Around and around I went, down, down, down. The garage had numerous columns painted yellow from the floor to about five feet up the concrete pillars so they were easy to see, and we parked the cars in slots between the columns.

One night, I raced up to an elegant elderly couple that arrived in a new baby blue Buick Electra. I gave them their ticket and waved my best customer service goodbye as they strolled arm in arm into the hotel. I gently eased myself behind the wheel and gingerly coasted out of the drive headed for the garage.

Harlow Curtice, former president of the Buick Division of General Motors, named this beauty after his sister-in-law, Electra Waggoner-Biggs. Harlow went on to become the president of GM, and the Buick Electra enjoyed a thirty-plus year run before it was replaced in 1991 with the Buick Park Avenue. Smiling ever so proudly and oozing the essence of testosterone, I turned into the garage, picked up speed on the downhill ramp, and wrapped the Baby Blue around a yellow cement column.

The front quarter panel, the driver's side door, and a bit beyond had a new yellow racing stripe, some visible metal under the paint, and a long unsightly dent. Scheduled to be off shift when the pair retrieved their newly renovated Buick, I breathed easier. Not inheriting the luck of the Irish; or any luck for that matter; the stately couple did not check into the hotel but were there to attend an event ending before my shift was over. The supervisor on duty gave me the insurance forms, directed me to deliver the car and inform the owners that I had, in fact, been the one who saw fit to pretzel their car around a pillar.

The well-dressed, happy, and classy couple called for their car around 11:00 p.m., and I had damaged the vehicle around 7:00 p.m. That allowed plenty of time to sweat it out. I drove out of the garage, around the hotel, and up the U-shaped drive to the entrance. I was pleased the driver's side faced the street, not the entrance to the hotel, so Mr. Classy didn't immediately see the damage. I parked and raced around the car, thinking if I intercepted him and told him before he saw the yellow stripe, it would go easier on me. He thought I was racing to open the door for his wife, and said, "I got it, young man. Don't concern yourself." In this era, chivalry wasn't dead, and the gentleman opened the door for his lady.

He headed around the front of the car and handed me a few folded bills as a tip. Now I'm standing there with a handful of insurance papers and his tip. I say, "Sir? Sir, I need to talk to you." The urgency and high pitch of my voice caused him to stop, thank goodness. I told him there was a minor incident with his car. Of course, he wanted the details, and I could not come up with a gentle way to say I wrapped your beautiful new car around a pole. He came around the car, surveyed the damage, and asked if I thought the accident would in any way interfere with the performance of the vehicle. I assured him the damage was cosmetic only because I wasn't going that fast. He said, "Fine," then slid into the driver's seat and took off. I was standing there dumbfounded with the tip held out toward the departing car—sure I shouldn't keep it. I got two extra bucks for wrecking the Electra. The Buick Electra may have had a thirty-year run, but in my hands, it didn't last thirty minutes.

I was enrolled in the College of Social Studies at Michigan State University, studying psychology when they threatened to toss me due to low grades. Psychology was easy for me, but getting to class was more difficult. Faced with expulsion, I switched to the only college that would take me—the College of Agriculture. Now I am many things but not a tiller of the soil. I worked very hard to get back into psychology and kept the grade point average above 3.0 until graduation.

Graduation 1967

I left Michigan State with a bachelor of science degree in psychology, a five-thousand-dollar debt, and a commission in the US Navy. My commission landed me in Vietnam where I could not smell the aromas of the kitchen, where I could not hear the cars whoosh by as I tried to sell them newspapers, where I could not shake the apple tree or duck when I heard "fore." Instead, I heard sirens and rockets. I smelled fear, and the only thing shaking was me and the people around me.

* * *

Somewhere Over the Gulf of Tonkin (1969)

With my ground duty over, I flew missions over the Gulf of Tonkin, putting my training from Pensacola to good use. We were on routine recon missions, flying in a Navy EC-121 Warning Star long-range reconnaissance aircraft. Adapted from the Lockheed Super Constellation, the aircraft had a fuselage radar system and numerous other electronic surveillance equipment on board. Our mission, to monitor electronic transmission and to act as a warning device for attacks on US resources, was vital.

There were two senior-level positions on the plane. The lead pilot who was responsible for the safe operation of the plane. He was in charge during takeoff and landing, and the senior electronic warfare evaluator, responsible for ensuring a successful reconnaissance effort. During my deployment to the Far East, it was decided that the lead pilot, referred to as the commander, was in charge during takeoff and landing and for any flight-related or mechanical issues. Once on station for the mission, the pilot turned over command of the aircraft and mission to the senior electronic evaluator. That was my role. Skip, our pilot, and I shared those responsibilities. We both respected each other's ability and trusted we would not overstep our area of expertise and would not put the aircraft and crew in danger.

We were flying north over the gulf when radar and electronic intercepts revealed the takeoff of a MiG-21 from Hanoi. Designed by the Mikoyan-Gurevich Design Bureau in the Soviet Union, this airborne weapons system is the most produced supersonic jet aircraft in aviation history since the Korean War. Sixty countries over four continents have flown the MiG-21. It still serves many nations a half century after its maiden flight.

The flight of the MiG was not unusual, and there was initially no cause for alarm. The North Vietnamese fighter began heading in a southerly direction. We were headed north. Not a good combination. Still, no cause for intense alarm; concern, yes; alarm, no. We had seen aircraft like this fly south of Hanoi for a few miles, then do a one-eighty and land back at Hanoi. Maybe the pilot forgot his compass because he continued south way beyond what we had seen before and what we expected.

Another North Vietnamese air base at Vinh, a considerable distance south of Hanoi and closer to the DMZ, may have been his destination.

If Hanoi was relocating a jet fighter to Vinh, there had to be a specific reason. This caused confusion and uncertainty with me and my crew. The speeding enemy jet, over land, and my plane, over the water, were mere minutes apart. What was their objective? Skip came back and looked over my shoulder. I briefed him on the situation and whispered a recommendation. I suggested he man the left seat and immediately turn to a southerly course away from the approaching MiG. The pilot in the left seat had command of the aircraft and was responsible for taking any necessary actions to keep us safe by following the appropriate protocol. We were under strict orders not to give up our EC-121 and all its secrets.

Russia, China, or Russian-trained forces, on occasion, flew up to US aircraft and signaled, tipping their wings up and down, to force our planes to follow them to an enemy-controlled air base. If you didn't follow, they threatened to shoot you down. We would not land our plane in enemy territory, and we certainly didn't want to be shot down. The MiG-21's air-to-air missile system was less effective at lower altitudes, so an evasive strategy was to descend to a lower altitude. In extreme cases, we were to ditch the aircraft in the ocean rather than turn it over to the enemy. Everyone knew this and tensions were high.

I listened to every bit of electronic information available but still couldn't determine the Mig-21's objective. I felt in my gut it did not plan to shoot us down. Of course, the EC-121 crew probably had the same thought in 1969 when the North Koreans shot it down while flying over the Sea of Japan. Thirty-one American lives were lost. Same mission. Same rock. Same hard place.

The North Vietnamese fighter continued south and then turned east toward us. Time to act. We had just minutes until the jet intercepted us. I called the aircraft carrier, patrolling in the Gulf of Tonkin and requested fighter back up immediately. We all knew they would never get to us in time. My only hope was that North Vietnam did not want to lose one of its few fighter aircraft and that launching the carrier's F-4s Phantom jets would deter the aggressor. McDonnell Douglas designed the F-4's as all-weather, long-range supersonic jet interceptor aircraft. Introduced into the Navy in 1960, the Phantom proved itself to be a highly adaptable weapon system and was later adopted by the Marine Corps and the Air Force.

I watched and listened to the activity, and I knew the other thirty-one men on this mission were watching and listening to me. I would give the order to ditch the aircraft, if necessary, and Skip in the left seat would not hesitate. Fear overcame me again, and tensions were off the charts.

Ken, my number 2, sat at the plotting table behind me. I manned the control console. My radar operator, Arky, sat beside me on his console, and we fired up every piece of equipment available to continue monitoring the situation. I attempted to hide my fear and remain in command. Looking up, I saw a young man sitting at the station located at my eleven o'clock position. He turned in his seat and looked me in the eyes. I saw in him all the fear I was desperately trying to mask. It rocked my boat. I knew the fear, felt the fear, and now I saw it reflected in his eyes. He was probably only nineteen or twenty, and I was significantly older at twenty-four. I gave him a thumbs-up sign to assure him we were okay, then signaled him to turn around and keep monitoring his frequency. I didn't know if the thumbs-up assurance was true or not.

The MIG-21 continued its trajectory toward us, and now the minutes to reach us diminished to seconds. The North

Vietnamese pilot turned on his air-to-air missile system, and the unmistakable *beep, beep, beep* of this system searching for a target to lock on caused many to think we were doomed. In my headphones, I heard crew members telling me to take the plunge. I heard the radio jabber of our fighter jets racing toward us and relaying their ETAs. The MiG would reach us first if that was his objective.

All our collective electronic intelligence, all I'd seen, all the input and interpretations, plus my own intuition told me his goal was not to shoot us down. I just could not be sure. The landing pattern at the Vinh air base could potentially be the flight path the MiG was flying. I believed he had exaggerated his approach pattern and activated his weapons systems just to scare us. But I could not sit at nine thousand feet and let my aircraft and crew become victims of an attack. What if I was wrong?

I communicated with Skip, telling him we were in a very precarious situation. I also relayed that I did not want him to take extraordinary action endangering the crew. I requested he begin a descent immediately—a slow and controlled descent, not an evasive and desperate plunge toward the sea. We would do that if we were under attack, but I told him I did not think we were under attack. If I was wrong, though, we would lose thirty-two lives, including mine. Wrong can mean doing nothing and get shot down. Wrong could also mean telling Skip to ditch the aircraft, and we still lose thirty-two lives. No one was likely to get out of this behemoth before it sank.

Welcome to That Rock and a Hard Place

Skip pushed the nose over. The plane began a controlled descent, and everyone knew I had given the order. You could see, smell, and hear the silent expression of fear, but everyone stood or sat firm and manned their positions. Arky had the enemy aircraft on radar, calling out his location, distance from us, and the seconds it would take to reach us. Those monitoring the enemy's electronic signals called out his actions as he began arming his weapons and getting us in his sights. Skip called out the changing altitude as we descended rapidly. Too rapidly for this aircraft, we called a bucket of bolts. The friendly forces on their way were still too far away to intervene in time.

Apple Pie and Tomorrow Were Not Guaranteed Anymore

At the last second, the MiG did a one-eighty and flew west to land at Vinh. He may have accomplished his mission if it was just to scare the crap out of us. I practically yelled at Skip to level off and return to altitude. The collective sigh of relief from the crew could have provided the lift we needed to return to nine thousand feet.

I stayed at the control console until I was sure the fighter aircraft had landed, turned off its engines and all its electronics systems. Only then did I know we were safe. I told Skip to return to the mission orbit, which meant going in the opposite direction of our southerly, evasive path—head north and continue the mission. I leaned behind me and told Ken to replace me at the control console. He took off his headset, stood, and gave me room to stand and move past him to the plotting table.

I Could Not Move

I was paralyzed from the waist down from fear. My flight suit, now half off and tied around my waist, was drenched. My legs did not work. Instead of standing and walking, I shuffled back to the plotting table using just my hands and any momentum I could muster. I sat at the table and acted like

I was reviewing the charts depicting the recent activity. I just held my head in my hands with my eyes closed, trying to reestablish equilibrium. It did not happen. I got hotter and hotter. I sweated more and more. I saw bright flashes like someone was turning a spotlight on and off behind my lids. I could not breathe, and I thought *this is the big one*. Twenty-four, and I was about to have a heart attack right here in front of my crew at nine thousand feet.

Suddenly, I heard Arky cry out, "Lieutenant, look!" He pointed under the plotting table, where I sat, to the power supply for the radar that had been running full tilt for hours. The power supply was on fire. The heat causing me to sweat so much was from a fire only inches from my knees. The flashing lights in my eyes were the glowing elements of the power supply blinking bright one moment and dim the next. I could not breathe because the aircraft was filled with smoke. That gray smoke again. Alarm raced through the crew, our aircraft was on fire, but I just laughed. The crew looked at me like I had a screw loose, but I felt so relieved about not having a heart attack.

Look for the Silver Lining

We had just survived a near-fatal encounter with a MiG-21 only to catch fire at nine thousand feet. Let's hope bad luck doesn't come in threes. We shut down all the equipment, vented the smoke out of the aircraft, and aborted our mission. We landed safely at Da Nang later that evening. I drank to celebrate and to remove the lasting vestiges of the fear. But celebrate what? We did the right thing, or did I celebrate that Dad was wrong? *I am not a coward, I am not stupid, and I can make good decisions.* I didn't celebrate heroics—just that I had begun challenging those old tapes in my head. I spent most of my life trying to be the son, the brother, the friend, the husband, or the soldier he wanted. I just never thought I measured up. I never understood it was okay to be afraid. I thought it made me weak, and I didn't want him to see me as weak. I was afraid to tell him I was human. We all walked through fear and survived; we didn't get paralyzed into inaction, and we didn't run. Maybe I didn't run because I was paralyzed from the waist down (LOL).

Chapter Two

CONTROVERSY

Before I even leave (1968)

Everything's a controversy. Being at home, going to Vietnam, and being me. It all seemed so difficult.

In December 1968, after I had shipped out, the world as I knew it ended.

What should have been a simple life turned very difficult. The difficulties were not just being in Vietnam, but what happened getting there and then coming home. I wonder who I would have become if I had been stationed in the peaceful hills of Europe and not the brown flatlands and swampy rice paddies of Vietnam.

The difficulties getting to Vietnam included fighting the controversy at home and working hard to get stationed elsewhere. I lost both battles.

The controversy at home consisted of more than just the national protests about the war. Home was love based—brotherly love, not a clash of political ideologies or the angry protests aimed at the "warmongers." My brother Billy was a protester. He was one of the leaders of the Students for a Democratic Society (SDS), protesting the United States involvement in Vietnam. I believe if Billy's number had come up in the draft, he would have headed for Canada. He would have been among the estimated five hundred thousand men labeled "draft dodgers" who fled the United States. Most headed to Canada, to avoid conscription. I saw his packed bag. He had determined not to go to Vietnam. Kent State University, Billy's alma mater, was his second choice for a college. His first choice, Penn State, kicked him out when he refused to join the ROTC program.

I enrolled in a program called AVROC (Aviation Reserve Officer Candidate). Not associated with Michigan State University, my training was unique and not like ROTC programs. I trained for my military career during the summer in Pensacola, Florida, and worked toward my bachelor's degree at Michigan State during the winter. I was commissioned and awarded my wings on the day I graduated from college. My military career started that day.

Swearing in Ceremony 1967

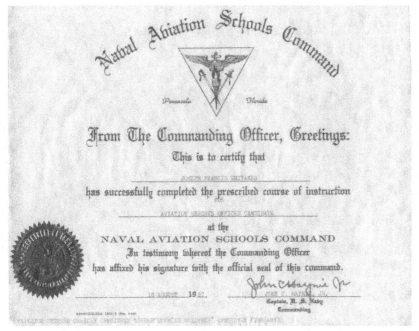

Certificate of Completion

My first assignment, Operation Feedback, sent me to the geographic area where I grew up and attended school. My mission required me to go from college to college in the Ohio-Michigan area to recruit more students to join the AVROC Program. Uncle Sam sent three million men to wage this war. The extremely high death rate of our soldiers in Vietnam, and the five hundred thousand men dodging to Canada and other locales, left us in dire need of new recruits.

Hands up

Ensign Joseph F. Whitaker, USNR, administers the oath to two future MSU Naval Aviation Officer Candidates, Christopher J. Witkoski, Edmor, senior (left), and Guy R. Horanberg, Lockport, N.Y., senior. State News photo by Mike Beasley

New Recruits

We stood behind six-foot tables handing out literature about the AVROC program and actively attempted to recruit. Large groups of protesters gathered on the other side of the tables handing out anti-war leaflets. Billy led a few of these efforts. Their goal was to block the entrance to the student unions and the approach to our tables. The protesters chanted and yelled so loud we couldn't converse with prospective candidates. They effectively shut us down. I was dressed in blues, and Billy in the hippy garb of the sixties, unshaven, wearing loose clothes of earth tones and an angry expression. Angry that we took men's rights away, forced men to go to war and, most importantly, fought an unjust war.

What a contradiction. Loving and caring about someone and being caught in the divide of one of our nation's worst controversies. Not since the civil war had we seen brother against brother with Americans dying because of their philosophical differences. What made matters worse, some these deaths occurred on our own soil at Kent State. We lost fifty-five thousand men on Vietnamese soil; we didn't need to lose any more at home.

We had, as a nation, previously disagreed with those in power. This effort differed in the strength and conviction of those opposed to our government. The new passionate and aggressive protest was founded in the belief they could change the edicts of our administration. Cries of "bring home the troops" and "end the war" rang out across our nation and in the student unions where I faced down with my brother. In the end, the protesters won, and those who fought lost.

The year 1967 was to be my last Christmas before being shipped out to Vietnam. Maybe it was to be my last Christmas forever. We were all gathered at the family home in Bradford, Pennsylvania. The family had accepted the fact that I was going to the war within a year. We tried to act normal, whatever that was. Christmas with tons of siblings was a festive occasion driven by the young anticipating Santa's visit, relatives coming in from all parts of the United States and the picture-perfect setting of the white snow-covered mountains in Northern Pennsylvania.

On Christmas morning, the young woke early and huddled in the hall, waiting for the older siblings and Mom and Dad to wake. They were not supposed to wake us. They were supposed to wait quietly until we opened our eyes naturally. That was the plan. The little ones hiding in the hall had their own scheme. They whispered loudly, walked up and down the hall of the second story where their little feet stomped heavily on the wooden floor. The echoes of the whispering and the footfalls could be heard in the north pole.

Finally, we all woke up and headed downstairs. Some moved quickly, and some moved ever so slowly, but everyone possessed an air of excitement. We turned the corner into the living room and saw the tree lit up in its full majesty, ten to twelve feet tall. Piles of wrapped packages lay under, around, and near the tree. Santa's dish of snacks had only a scattering of crumbs on it, and his glass of milk was almost empty. Proof positive he had visited the night before. I think I heard sleigh bells from high above.

Dad sat under the tree and passed out the packages one by one, which just magnified the anticipation and excitement. We all sat and watched each other as a gift was given and opened slowly. The "ohs" and "aahs" and whoops of joy filled the three-story house.

Magical

Billy's gift to me that year was his last-ditch effort to convince me of his position on the war. We found a quiet moment and had a private conversation in the living room.

Billy said, "I don't understand why you feel so strongly that you must go. This conflict is a byproduct of US imperialism and not a war to liberate Vietnam or keep the peninsula free of Communism. The United States is supporting a failing dictatorship in South Vietnam, and it is not our war." He said our government was forcing young men into danger not based on prurient ideals but on a blatant desire for power. He debated how the outcome had no benefit to the United States and how painful the losses would be.

I responded with my patriotism and my belief in my country right or wrong. I still believed in the ideals of morality and democracy as the foundations of our foreign policy.

He saw that his logic, his intellectual opposition to the United States' decision in Indochina to engage in this war, and his overwhelming desire for peace were not going to work.

So he tried love.

He begged me not to go to war. "You're my brother, and I love you. Don't go. I don't want those painful losses we were talking about to end up on our doorstep."

That didn't work either. I had to go. I had to prove to Dad I wasn't a coward and a failure. I was determined to be the son, the brother, the husband, and soldier that I believed I needed to be.

The "before" photo

Training

After the controversy at home, the second and parallel challenge that I encountered was in flight school. There were two openings for the specialty I was trained for; one in Spain with Fleet Air Reconnaissance Squadron Two, VQ-2, and one in Japan with Fleet Air Reconnaissance Squadron One, VQ-1, which operated in support of the Vietnam War. VQ1's squadron headquarters was in Atsugi, Japan. Those stationed there would fly in and out of Vietnam. Since they were based in Japan, their families could live overseas. Those assigned to VQ-1 would be part of a crew "in-country," which meant in Vietnam for three to four weeks at a time and then return to Atsugi. In Japan, these crews would conduct missions over the Sea of Japan and monitor activity in Northeast Asia before returning to Vietnam. Given the nature of the assignment the training required, and the fact that the crews flew back and forth between Vietnam and Japan, the tour was scheduled for three years.

The mission, for my specialty, was to gather data, through electronic surveillance, on the enemy's potential threats and provide early warnings for surface-to-air and air-to-air attacks on our forces. The selection process for our assignment to a squadron was simple: whomever graduated first in the class got his choice of assignment. (I say "his" because women were not allowed in combat roles in the 1960s. It would be many years before that bias was overcome.) I studied hard and worked hard and graduated first in my class. Named battalion chief, I led the class, wearing our navy dress whites, across the parade ground to receive our wings. Mom and Dad came down from Pennsylvania for the graduation and presented me my sword on which they had engraved my name. It was a proud day. The Florida heat and humidity didn't deter our pride, and I still have the picture of me in whites, Mom in a green floral dress with a matching pillbox hat, and Dad in a suit. It was a proper wear for the sixties and for the proper family from the northeast.

Military graduation

Mom and Dad (Pensacola, Florida, 1967)

The damper on the day came when we were advised that the billet in Spain had been canceled. The needs of war and the demands from Southeast Asia were far more pressing, so the opening for a recruit in Spain was reallocated to support the Vietnam conflict. The top two students were assigned to VQ-1 in Japan. So much for hard work and dedication.

Welcome to reality in wartime.

Chapter Three

THE GOLD DIGGER

In college, I dated Doris. We met at Michigan State. Nine days after I met her, I asked her to marry me. I'm a bit impetuous. We waited a year and a half, and that showed some rationality. But when you don't have a good perspective on who you are, rationality doesn't really help.

We met in the basement canteen located between our dorms at Abbot Hall and Mason Hall, an early experiment in coed dorms in the 1960s. The men's hall, Abbot, on one side, and the women's hall, Mason, on the other side. They shared a common central lobby and reception area on the first floor, and the canteen, study areas, and hang out spots on the lower level. Doris sat with a few friends in the corner, laughing, drinking Coke, and having a good time when I ambled into the crowd. I immediately asked to sit with them, and we all became friends. One of the freshmen bragged on Doris's impersonation of Carol Channing. They all demanded that she do her little skit. She tried to beg off, but they kept insisting. We all encouraged, cajoled, and eventually forced Doris to do her imitation of Carol. Under the pressure and spotlight of her peers, the impersonation bombed big-time. She really could do a stand-up version of Carol, but not this time. Undaunted, I asked Doris if we could see each other again, and she consented.

In October 1966, I proposed, and we made two promises. First, I promised to buy her a ring as soon as I could, but it probably wouldn't be for a while as we were starving students. At least I was. Her family was well off, and I think her dad thought I was a gold digger. Second, we promised not to tell anyone just yet. The time frame of "just yet" wasn't defined, and we agreed that I would meet the future in-laws, Regina and Chet, at Thanksgiving that same year.

Meet the Families

I drove my green 1952 Plymouth Selecto-matic to Detroit to visit and be introduced to my future family. The Plymouth had one of the first automatic transmission, and I was a proud owner. My very first ever car bought with my hard-earned wages from the doughnut shop, the car wash, and smashing up perfectly good cars at the Jack Tar Hotel. I called it the Jolly Green Giant. The Giant, however, had some warts.

The car had two significant problems. First, the car only selectively started. On those occasions when the Giant didn't purr to life on command, my college mates and I leaped, undaunted, from the car and pushed it to get it going. Sometimes someone with another vehicle pushed it until the Giant leaped to life. Once started, we were always treated to a thick cloud of white smoke. When I turned off the car, we were treated to that same thick cloud of white smoke, accompanied by the coughing and sputtering of the engine. It reminded me of someone expiring from a bad cough.

The second problem was there was no reverse gear. Not a showstopper. I just couldn't back up utilizing engine power. We had to again jump out of the car and push it backward into parking spaces and out of tight spots. One day, my friends and I pushed the car into an oncoming vehicle and caused some damage. The owner was not pleased because he couldn't believe a bunch of college kids had hit him with a hand-pushed car. Annoyed because of the damaged car and annoyed because the people responsible were slightly tipsy and laughing at the unbelievable turn of events, he called the cops.

An officer of the law promptly arrived at the scene of the "crime." I told the officer my side of the story, the truth. I said, "Officer, my friends and I were pushing the Jolly Green Giant into the parking structure. We had to push it because there is no reverse. I have class early tomorrow morning, and no one will be up that early to help me push it out of the parking space. If we don't back it into the space tonight, I'm stranded. This car is huge. Our heads were down while pushing, and we lost control of the Giant. It hit the oncoming vehicle."

The cop looked at me, looked at the owner of the damaged vehicle, and tried hard to keep a straight face, and then he lost it. He laughed so hard he doubled over in hysteria, turned, and walked away to regain his composure. The victim in this crime did not appear happy. I did not get cited. I don't think he knew how to write up that an unmanned vehicle caused such a scene, and he couldn't find a traffic code for lack of reverse.

I drove my priceless Giant to Detroit to meet the in-laws oblivious of a lurking problem. Daddy-in-law-to-be, an executive with the Ford Motor Company, and I, as the proud owner of a Plymouth, represented a product betrayal of serious magnitude. They lived in the beautiful estate-filled enclave of Bloomfield Hills. His ranch-style house sat back from the road on a slight rise with a long horseshoe-shaped driveway arching through meticulous landscaping. The front of the house was accented by a mammoth picture window. My first impression was of green lushness oozing pomp and grace from every shrub and flower bed. As I graced the drive in my 1952 Plymouth, I saw my intended and her parents through the picture window patiently awaiting my arrival. They came to the ornate double paneled front door to greet me just as I shut down the growling Giant.

At that precise moment, problem number one resurrected its ugly head. The Giant coughed and sputtered, shook and rattled, rocked forward and backward but never moved an inch. The cloud of white smoke began to wash over the greeters obscuring them from view. The ornate front door slammed loudly. Father-in-law-to-be hustled everyone back into the safe interior of the house, thinking the beast was about to explode. I sat lost in swirling smoke. I heard the sputtering of the car, the echo of the unmanned door knocker banging out an angry tune, and the windowpanes rattling in their frames. I was sure this was not an omen of happy forever after.

I had no sense of direction and had to grope around in the white haze to locate the front door, knock, and request admission to the mansion. "Dad's" first words were "take that thing around back *now*." I dutifully drove my car around the U-shaped drive and down the hill behind the house and out of sight, ever so grateful that in this edgy situation, the Giant started on command.

I entered the home through the garage (or was it the servant's entrance) and settled in the chair directly in front of the in-laws. Doris looked grim-faced, dad-in-law wore a very stern face, and mom-in-law was trying hard not to laugh. She looked like the cop who lost it at my "accident." She loved it. We were kindred spirits. The second salvo from dear ole dad was, "So I understand you want to marry my daughter."

The time frame for "not just yet" promised when I asked Doris to marry me became defined that moment. I squirmed, twisted, and slid back and forth in the oversize, overstuffed, designer chair, *all I needed now was to ruin the furniture.* Everything looked brand new and unused. In my house only scuff marks were new. I stuttered out an answer that still eludes me to this day. We spent an awkward day or two together and, eventually, began the goodbye process. I wanted to head home to Pennsylvania for the rest of the holiday.

I packed up the Giant, located behind the house, and to my deep chagrin, the Giant did not start. With help, I pushed the car up to the street and asked Ford Dad for assistance to get my pride and joy started. That took guts, but innocence and naivete were strong suits in those days. Dad swung his little new rose-colored T-Bird up from the garage and inched it up to the rear bumper of the Jolly Green Giant. I wondered if rose and green would blend well to create an eye-pleasing shade? I did not want an answer to that random thought.

I, in the driver's seat, and Doris, in the passenger seat, said our Victorian goodbyes waiting for dad-in-law to pull up behind us. Suddenly there was a rapping on the passenger window. Doris rolled down the window. Yes, rolled down the window. Nothing was automatic on this car, except the transmission—if you were going forward. When the window was about halfway, Dad leaned in and said to Doris, "Get out of the car, *now.*" He liked saying "now." I sneaked one last quick peck on the cheek before Doris leaped from the Plymouth into the T-Bird.

Bumpers touched ever so gently, and the vehicles start parading down the tree-lined streets. Serenity prevailed. But I wasn't breathing. I was praying dearly to the god of old motors, "Please start. Please start." There was no clutch to pop; with an automatic transmission, it's pure chance. But with a glorious cough, the Giant surged to life. I cranked down the window, stuck my hand out and waved an ever so grateful thank you. I didn't dare to stop within sight of the in-laws.

I wanted to ensure they acknowledged my gratitude. I looked in my rearview mirror as I sped off into the sunset and was greeted with a vision of thick white smoke. I thought I saw two human silhouettes sitting in the vehicle behind me. The driver's head appeared to be moving left and right in nonverbal disapproval or just disbelief.

* * *

The day arrived when Doris planned to travel to Bradford, Pennsylvania, to meet my family. Turnabout is fair play. She had one brother and one sister, but what awaited her was a bit intimidating. She had to embed herself with my six brothers, three sisters, Mom and Dad, and whatever animals lingered about the house. In anticipation of the meet and greet, a home-cooked dinner was scheduled for her first evening in Pennsylvania. Doris decided to wear a beautiful new gray cashmere sweater adorned with a simple strand of pearls. To complete this look, Doris had traveled throughout Europe and Great Britain, shopping for a matching gray cashmere skirt. She finally located exactly what she wanted in London. She looked regal and radiant. Her long dark hair reached almost to her shoulders. The gray sweater and skirt, black shoes, and white pearls were accompanied by a dazzling smile. She descended the carpeted stairs and gracefully entered the big dining room where everyone waited for her arrival. She sat down, looked up, and twenty-four eyes were fixed on her every move, twenty-four ears tuned to hear her every word, and the most awkward silence hung like a cloud in the air.

Mom's menu for the occasion consisted of spaghetti and meatballs in red sauce. Not Irish but very tasty. The aromas of simmering meatballs and stewing tomato sauce wafted from the kitchen. Mom had cooked a huge vat of pasta and an immense pot of meat sauce. The meal was ladled from the various pots onto plates in the kitchen. Mom appointed brother Steve to be the steward. As Mom piled the pasta, meat, and sauce onto individual plates, Steve had orders to deliver each plate to the dining room and place it in front of the designated diner. Steve had a bit of the dramatic flair. The drama peaked as he delivered Doris's portion. He raised the plate, perched on fingertips, high above his head and, with the panache of Clark Gable, swung it from above the right side of his head in a counterclockwise movement, attempting to land the plate on the place mat in front of Doris. He stopped the plate's movement mere inches from the table to ensure proper placement.

Timing and physics are everything. Steve lacked awareness of momentum and its consequences. He didn't calculate that the mound of spaghetti would not stop when the plate did. The food on the now-stationary plate kept moving, sliding in a sinister blob until the pile of pasta, meatballs, and red sauce arched off the plate and down Doris's front, coming to rest in her gray cashmere lap.

I looked to my right, and I saw the pasta, red sauce, meatballs, and a look that would stop a freight train. I really tried to be empathetic and sad and chagrined, but when I looked a second time, there was an array of noodles dangling off Doris's ample boobs. The sight was slapstick humor at its best. I started laughing. I could not stop laughing, and it mortified Doris even more. She bolted from the table and raced upstairs to her room. I looked up to see Steve frozen in place like a statue. Mom leaning against the doorframe of the dining room, shaking her head with her hand covering her face, and Dad turning bright red with anger. The remaining sixteen sets of eyes were agog with shock and fear. I thought Dad was angry at Steve, but instead, he yelled at me for laughing. I got a lecture on how inappropriate it was to laugh. I was sure that was going to be the end of our budding romance, but Doris, forgiving and gracious, moved beyond the incident successfully.

The Best-Laid Plans

In March 1967, I decided to buy Doris that ring I threatened her with. I saved the money I made at odd jobs over the holidays, the fall semester, and the first few months of the winter semester. I found a small but beautiful ring. I wish I could have done better; she deserved it. Being a romantic at heart, I devised a plan to surprise her.

I invited a few friends over for her high-class birthday dinner of pizza and beer. Dessert was a small chocolate cake suitable for the occasion and the budget. Using a clear capsule that must have contained a pocket-size toy for a child, I stuffed it with cotton and placed the ring in the cotton. The capsule opened from the middle. When she popped open the capsule, hopefully, the ring would be visible sitting up peeking out of the cotton and sparkling in the fluorescent light of the dorm room. One final step, I hid the ring capsule inside the cake. Cutting a plug out of the bottom of the cake, I inserted the capsule and replugged the hole. The cake, now right side up, needed some touch up on the frosting to ensure she wouldn't notice the surgical efforts that went into this surprise. We sang, she blew out the candles, and cut four or five small pieces of cake for the guests. To my chagrin, the capsule remained in the uncut portion of the cake. It was sticking out of the cake, visible to the others present, but on the side of the cake, facing away from Doris where she couldn't see it.

I quickly said, "Why don't you cut the rest of the cake, and if anyone wants seconds, it'll be ready for them?"

She politely declined and said they could cut it themselves. I said, "No, no. Let's be gracious hosts."

After a few rounds of yes, no, yes, no from the assertive duo, Doris reluctantly cut the remainder of the cake and the capsule fell onto the plate looking like a huge pill for a diarrheic cow. At first, she looked at it liked it was going to explode. She had a horrific grimace on her face that implied. "What is this?" She then popped the capsule amid the cheers and applause of our guests. The capsule separated in the middle, and the ring sparkled from its nest of cotton. It worked. She gasped in surprise, hugged me, and the rest of my plan came true. Sometimes plans do work with a little nudge.

During our engagement, I spent a few months in Pensacola, Florida, after graduating from Michigan State in 1967. Doris remained in East Lansing. I completed my military training and readied myself to be shipped overseas. A fun and hectic time—studying, planning a future, and not dwelling on any negative possibilities. I lived in Pensacola with a colleague named Andy. His career path and curriculum were different from mine, but we were close, and we shared the journey. I called Doris often, and she called me. Andy frequently got jealous because we were engaged, and he was not engaged to his longtime sweetheart, Elsie. One night, we were out drinking; actually we were out drunk, and Andy got so jealous he decided to rectify the situation on the spot. We were men of action, especially men of drunk action. Andy picked up the phone and, while still drunk, called Elsie and asked her to marry him.

It was the sixties, and we were singing songs like "Dedicated to the One I Love" by the Shirelles or "When a Man Loves a Woman" by Percy Sledge. We wanted to be good and work hard "For Your Precious Love" by the Impressions, and we wanted to be "So Much in Love" by the Tymes. An innocent time, a romantic time, and we believed in one special love. We were not singing "I'm Drunk, Let's Get Hitched" by Andy. We can safely say that song did not hit Elsie's top 10 on the Billboard charts.

Elsie became very upset. We worried that the rift between her and Andy might not heal but it was the sixties and one special love won the day. Elsie forgave Andy and eventually married him. They were together until 2015 when Elsie passed from cancer. Love does not conquer all, but it gives you a life full of memories and a life worth living.

Doris and I got married in June of 1968 in Bradford, Pennsylvania. I was leaving for Japan early that December. We married in my hometown because her parents lived overseas. On the Friday before our wedding, June 27, Mom insisted our family be professionally photographed. The photo was a staged, very formal iconic pose of the entire clan, Mom, Dad, and the ten children. This picture is a much-revered photo and is dragged out at all family reunions. No one knew that Mom's motivation was her fear I wasn't coming home.

Doris, not happy about taking the time out of the wedding planning for my family portrait, didn't share or understand Mother's viewpoint. When the arguments against the venture were not well received by the matriarch of the family, and I became ineffective at resolving it, Doris went over my head to Dad. He took Doris's side and tried to dissuade Mom from insisting that we sit for this portrait. Mom whispered her reason for the portrait to Dad, and I overheard her say, "This may be the last opportunity we'll all be together, especially with Joey going to Vietnam. He might not come home."

When the photo was pulled out for grins and giggles at reunions, I see something entirely different. It's hard to smile and look happy and pleasant when you know the photo is being taken because you might not be alive at the next family gathering.

Family photo (June 1968)

When I look at the portrait now, it's not like looking in a mirror and seeing myself staring back. I don't recognize the person I used to be. It is an ominous feeling. There is little recognition of what used to be.

Doris and I were married the next day.

Wedding day (June 1968)

Doris and Joe with Nanas May (L) and Josephine (R)

We visited relatives in New York for a weekend and then went back to Pensacola to finish training. We sneaked away for a few days to have a honeymoon in New Orleans, but by December, I shipped out to Japan. We were advised that we would have to live off base because there was no available base housing. The Far East was a staging area for the war, and it became overcrowded. Living off base was referred to as living "on the economy."

I found a two-bedroom house not designed with Bloomfield Hills in mind. The only heat came from a potbellied stove in the middle of the living room. Exposed ducting hanging from the ceiling dispersed heat to the other rooms. I arrived a month before Doris and set up the house for her arrival. Some nights it was so cold I wrapped myself in a blanket and slept in the mudroom. The mudroom was a small entryway where people took off their shoes before entering the living area. We all followed that custom in Japan out of respect for our hosts. The enclosed shoe closet was so small my body heat kept me warm.

While I suffered overseas setting up the household, Doris stayed with my family in Bradford. I'm not sure who suffered more, and I'm pretty sure that leaving Doris in the clutches of my family wasn't one of my wiser decisions. Bill and Jane, my mother and father, eight children still at home and probably a dog or two were Doris's new housemates. If that wasn't punishment enough, add to the mix the grandmonster from hell. Grandma was sweet and nice to me because I was one of her favorites. No one used the term or knew what high maintenance meant in that era. Today, Grandma's picture is in the dictionary as the personification of high maintenance.

Nana May McCann and her "favorite"

Mom's mom, May McCann, was on the sibling tour. A sibling tour is May going from one of her kids to another throughout the year. Segments of the tour were determined by how long the host family could handle May or, in the case of my dad, how long May could stand him.

May's husband, Frank, had passed on, and the finances did not allow for May to have her own staff to boss around, so we got the honors. Grandpa Frank was the rock in May's world. Calm as the day was long with a well of patience that never seemed to go dry, the caretaker from heaven, Frank took care of everything. One day, Frank woke up, paid all the bills, canceled an order for a new couch, headed off to work at Lincoln Downs, a racetrack in Rhode Island, and never came home. Grampy was an electrician at the raceway, and he kept the lights on. That day, his light flickered with a massive heart attack. He must have known it was coming, and that's why he paid the bills, canceled the new couch, and got the financial paperwork in order so Nana wouldn't have to do it. Frank was rushed to the hospital in critical condition, where he lingered for a short period of time as if he was waiting for something or some signal to let go. Mom flew to Rhode Island later that night and raced into his hospital room. She was greeted by the words "Oh, my Janie's here. I can go now," and Frank left us that moment.

Grampy Frank's typical Irish Catholic wake was held in a funeral home owned by relatives in Providence, Rhode Island. The clan gathered for the viewing all drank, argued, were rowdy, and disrespectful. It looked like a party to my ten-year-old self, and I found it sinful. Mom and Dad, preoccupied with details, didn't notice I had become upset. I just decided to leave. I didn't know where I was, feeling so down about the behavior of the grown-ups, I walked out onto the streets of Providence. Undaunted by the big city and the unfamiliar terrain, I descended the four or five cement steps, turned right on the sidewalk, and meandered down the boulevard. I had no idea what to do or where to go. I just knew I had to get out of there.

I sensed the presence of someone walking up behind me—Aunt Kitty, Katherine by birth. She had married Mom's brother Frank Jr. Kitty didn't say a word; she just walked with me. Kitty was beautiful, and she cared about me. Kitty had auburn hair with a pure wide white streak that went from her forehead over the crown of her head and blended with the silky long hair flowing to her neckline.

At her wedding to Frank Jr., she asked me to dance with her. She was in her wedding gown and I in my little boy suit. She made me feel so grown-up, so wanted, and so important. I loved Aunt Kitty. We walked in silence until she gently said, "It's really sad, isn't it?" I don't remember all we said, but it was enough. I let her know I was angry with the adults, and she didn't argue.

Eventually, she steered me back to the funeral home, and the festive ambiance didn't seem to bother me so much. It was nice to be a part of an extended family with people who could comfort me and understood me. I'm not sure Dad's challenging me or Mom's weeping and clutching me would have made the difference, but Aunt Kitty did. Aunt Kitty had MS and left us early. It seemed like another time and another world.

Frank Sr. was gone, and May made the rounds. May had a meddling and demanding nature. When the "you know what" hit the proverbial fan, May was either sent to her room to pack, or she went off in a huff. Either way, she was packing her suitcase. Mom got on the phone with her brother or sister to say it was time. They usually met this information with resistance. After a few rounds of "It's your turn" and "No, it's not. She just got to your place" or "Call your brother," my mother ended the argument with, "If you don't take her, all hell's going to break loose here." The unfortunate math in this situation is that May had only three kids. Why couldn't she have been the one to have ten?

In true style and just to be helpful, May decided to take responsibility to ensure Doris could take care of her grandson, Joey. May sat knitting in the family room with Doris reading nearby when the clothes dryer shut off. In a family with ten kids, that dryer was going all the time. The dinging of the alarm, alerting anyone interested that the cycle ended, did not bode well for Doris. The load contained sheets for some of the upstairs beds. May had it in her head that Doris, a bit spoiled, was used to people waiting on her day and night. May assumed she didn't know the ABCs of keeping house. May struggled out of the wingback chair—she wasn't tiny and dainty—and grabbed a handful of Doris's blouse near her shoulder and said, "Come on, missy, upstairs. I'm going to teach you how to make a bed correctly so you can take care of my Joey." I'm sort of glad I wasn't there because Doris may have given me back to May without a second thought.

When Doris arrived in Japan, we bought an electric blanket with dual controls. It was January, and the newlyweds didn't want to sleep in the mudroom. Nothing but top of the line for us—dual controls, mind you. Doris liked it warm, and I preferred it much cooler. On our first night using the blanket, I was dying of the heat, and she was freezing. I was taking clothes off. Doris was wearing pajamas, but she got up and put on a sweater, socks, a watch cap, and got back under the latest technological blanket and was still shivering. We finally figured out the problem. We had crossed the wires, and I had her control side on my side, and mine was on hers. When I cranked the blanket down, she froze. She cranked the blanket up, and I lost water weight by the gallon.

One day, Doris backed into the potbellied stove while it was blazing away, and she was not a happy camper. She scorched some sensitive body parts and ruined a new pair of slacks. Being with me was hard on her wardrobe. I did not keep her in the custom that she was used to. That was her second uncomfortable experience with Japan. Her first occurred when I picked her up at the airport. Driving home in heavy traffic, a car in front of us stopped, the door opened, and the male driver leaped out and ran toward the side of the road. We slammed on the brakes and watched as he whipped out his Johnson and peed. He made no attempt to hide his manhood and did all the things we usually do in private like examine it, shake it, wave it, and do the "proud owner" dance.

The men of Japan had a habit of stopping to relieve themselves in the drainage ditch by the side of the road. If you gotta go, you gotta go! The only time I lost it over this custom was when the guy in front of us apparently had an emergency. He slammed on his brakes, came to a stop, and raced from the car, leaving the door wide open. I had to stop abruptly to avoid hitting him. Debby, our firstborn, sat in the baby carrier on the seat between us. With the sudden pee stop, the baby carrier flew forward into the dashboard. Debby hit the dash, bounced back, slid down the base of the seat, and ended up on the floor between us.

I did little that day to advance relations between Japan and the United States and, in fact, what I called that guy might have set those relations back a bit. I was afraid for my child and operated on adrenaline when I jumped from the car and read him the riot act. It didn't escalate into an international incident that day, as he spoke no English, and I spoke no Japanese. He stood looking at me with his mouth agape, and his hand encircling his exposed "business." My yelling and presence in his space caused him to lose his urge to pee. I think I got my point across.

Doris taught the son of a Japanese auto dealer his second language, English. We learned this young man of eight or nine years old went to school for ten to twelve hours per day. He attended elementary classes from early morning to early evening, then proceeded to music training and, after that, went home to meet Doris for his English lesson. It took that kind of dedication to create a generation that changed Japan's manufacturing quality and earned it the lion's share of the electronic and auto industries. The family often invited us to dinner, and we absorbed some of the culture and learned valuable lessons about our host nation. However, some of the food scared me; I'm a meat-and-potatoes kind of guy, not accustomed to quail eggs, seaweed, raw tuna, and other unknown delicacies.

Doris also mastered the art of Ikebana, Japanese flower arranging. Simple, elegant designs that catch your eye and make you stare as if they were whispering a message to you. They had a story to tell. Ikebana is more than simply sticking flowers in a pot or vase. It's a disciplined art form which often emphasizes unusual parts of the plant, such as its stems and leaves. It also puts focus on shapes, lines, and forms. Though Ikebana is a creative expression, it has certain rules governing its form. The artist's intention behind each arrangement is shown through the design's color combinations, natural shapes, and graceful lines. This art form emphasizes minimalism. Arrangements may consist of only a minimal number of blooms interspersed among stalks and leaves. Not the traditional large arrangement of many blooms we often see in the United States. The container is also important to the composition, so careful selection of the pottery is integral to the finished piece.

* * *

Our first daughter, Debby, arrived eleven months after we were married, our second daughter, Julie, born ten months later, and our son, Matthew, born sixteen months after Julie caused Doris some concern. She had never agreed to duplicate the size of my family. Doris kept turning up my side of the electric blanket to see if it would keep me away from her.

There were lots of homecomings. I often left Japan, flew to Vietnam to be in country for three to four weeks, flew back to Japan for a couple of weeks, just to fly out again.

In 1969, the economy of Japan was weak. Our military salary made us comfortable, and we had two beautiful ladies help us with the housekeeping and babysitting—Tomika and Kyoko. Tomika-san came once a week to help clean the house. She was industrious and ambitious. She had no car but owned two bicycles. One, parked at her house some miles away, and the second parked at a rail station near us. Tomika rode her bike to the depot in her town, locked it up for the day, rode the train to our town, and then biked to our house. She worked all day and then did the bike-train trip back home. She did this several times a week for many military families, and she was happy to do it.

Kyoko-san lived by herself four or five blocks away, and Tomika referred her to us. A forty-something-year-old single woman, she loved to babysit for us. We didn't have phones, so when I needed a babysitter, I walked over unpaved dirt roads to Kyoko's house and knocked on her door. She answered quickly and always agreed to sit with the girls. We only had the two girls then. Sometimes I asked if she could come immediately, and she always answered yes. Kyoko loved the girls and doted on them. We all loved her too.

We paid Kyoko and Tomika in two ways. The monetary reimbursement agreed to by both parties, and that didn't amount to much, so Doris and I supplemented their pay with food from the commissary. Chicken, other meats, eggs, butter, and sweets were a special prize. They considered them a gift of the highest order. In Japan, if someone gave you a gift, by tradition, you had to return the gesture with a gift of higher value. Both ladies bought us nice treasures. It took time to convince them we considered the food items as part of their pay and not a gift. We had to be careful when giving things to our friends in Japan because respect, dignity, and tradition were important characteristics of this culture.

Our squadron moved from Japan to Guam. There, Doris and I spent our last year overseas. As we were planning to leave Japan, we asked Kyoko if she wanted to come with us to Guam and be our live-in nanny. Doris was pregnant with number three. Kyoko was alone, single, and dedicated to our children, and she quickly responded positively. If all went well and she was comfortable with us, at the end of the year, she could move on to the States. If Kyoko didn't like it or got homesick, she had the option to return to Japan. We promised to take care of all her expenses. With her enthusiastic yes, we began planning and packing.

Shortly after our conversations with Kyoko, unexpected callers came to our home. I answered the door to find a very well-dressed woman and two men in suits on the steps. The woman wore a coral skirt with matching jacket and a bright floral blouse. She looked very distinguished. The men stood behind her back in black and very quiet. She introduced herself as Kyoko-san's sister and the men as family lawyers. They requested our presence at a meeting scheduled for a week from that date. We agreed thinking it was to iron out the details of our arrangement with Kyoko.

Doris and I arrived at Kyoko's house to find her huddled in a corner of the room, teary-eyed, red-faced, and avoiding our gaze. The sister informed us, through interpreters, that we had to rescind our offer to take Kyoko with us to America. We didn't understand. Kyoko had been so excited about our offer. It didn't make sense. The sister informed us that Kyoko was "damaged goods." She had been born with a lung defect and was not suitable for our family. The reason Kyoko was a spinster and lived alone was because she was not considered suitable for marriage either. We argued and assumed responsibility for her health care as well, but nothing seemed to matter. The answer was no. We insisted she come with us because we saw Kyoko didn't agree with the sister and the band of lawyers. The meeting went from stiffly casual to urgently formal, and they informed us, if we persisted, we would be taken to court and forced to rescind our offer. We lost the battle and, amid tons of tears, left Japan sans Kyoko-san.

Guam, an island 32 miles long had some beautiful spots, but we were clearly the minorities there. The local islanders were territorial, turf oriented, and aloof. Labor was imported from other nearby islands or countries, and the US military was an unwelcome inhabitant of the island. Guam is a US territory, and the military kept it afloat, but we still felt like the enemy at home. It was clear that the white intruders were not seen as beneficial but more as unsuspecting victims the locals could prey upon.

Some islanders pulled a con job on us. They waited at a sharp curve in one of the narrow roads, and as our car approached, they threw a scrawny, half-dead chicken in front of us. With no warning and no time to stop, we hit the scarecrow-looking fowl and finished him off. As we got out of the car to inspect the deceased bird, our first thought was no big loss. You couldn't even make a stew with that scrawny thing. Then we were summoned to court because the owner of the thighs-and-legs claimed it was a prize cockfighter that was single-handedly responsible for earning the entire financial support of the large, large family. We paid. I wish we had cell phones back then. I would have taken a picture and shown the judge that this chicken with malnutrition couldn't even fart without help. We'd have probably lost anyway; the judges were part of the same culture.

On another occasion, a Navy petty officer rode a motorcycle along the island's only four-lane highway when he was struck by a vehicle moving at high speeds. He never saw the car coming. As the investigating officer, my responsibilities included determining if there any negligence on the part of our service member. The police had initially advised the commanding officer that our man was at fault. There was significant damage to the car, the petty officer's motorcycle, and his severe injuries would cause significant lost time from work. The car hit the motorcycle so hard it launched the sailor straight up into the air as if shot from a cannon. The force ripped the skin off the insides of his legs and dropped him brutally by the side of the road.

I immediately went to the police station and requested the accident report. Treated as an intruder again, I waited for hours. When I finally got the report and read it, I was shocked and furious. The first police officer on the scene had drawn a map that reflected an accurate portrayal of the accident. The car heading west, down from Nimitz Hill, turned right onto the four-lane highway. The motorcyclist, on the other side of the highway, drove north at or below the speed limit. The driver of the car intended to go north not south on the highway, but the heavy traffic made it tricky to turn left. To accomplish her objective, she turned right and then almost immediately flipped a bitch—a.k.a. a U-turn—right into the side of the oncoming motorcycle. This was depicted in the drawing on the report. The written portion of the report contradicted the map and the facts of the situation and blamed the driver of the motorcycle.

No investigation or follow-up to the initial report occurred. No toxicology report on the Guamanian driver could be found, and there was no mention of the condition of the Navy man, who was seriously hurt and clung to life in the hospital. The report, incorrectly, went on to list the only witness as a passenger in the lady's car. No charges were filed against the owner of the car, and I had to write an extensive rebuttal of the police report to ensure our injured serviceman did not have to shoulder the blame. Territorial justice was biased, limited, and tough to fight.

Welcome to Minority Status

We stuck to our own, took care of one another, and grew close with the Navy families on Guam. Doris and I lived atop Nimitz Hill, two doors down from Gary and Judy. We had the two girls, and Gary and Judy had one boy. When I deployed to Vietnam, Gary frequently stopped at our house and checked on Doris and the kids to see if they were doing well or to see if they needed anything. When Gary was away, I did the same for Judy. We hung out together, went to dinner together, and shared the burdens of being away from home and often separated. Too bad we don't do that today. I think today we don't even know our neighbors. We don't stop in to see how they are doing, and we don't bring casseroles over when they move into the neighborhood.

* * *

I think of the frequent violent attacks we experience in the United States these days. They are horrific. Some of these atrocities are blamed on "lone wolf" attackers. Homeland Security, the police, and all the intelligence available are not able to deter lone wolf attackers. The solution lies with every one of us, and we need to take care of each other like we did overseas. We need to know our community and what's going on in it.

To have bomb makers living next door, to have people stockpiling weapons for a mass shooting, or to have our neighbors sheltering an attack team with no one noticing is unimaginable. We see strange things and say nothing. Worse yet, we don't even know who lives in the houses our children pass by on their way to school. We are ultimately responsible, and if we do not live up to that responsibility, we may pay an ultimate price for our reclusive and self-absorbed ways. John F. Kennedy said, "Ask not what your country can do for you; ask what you can do for your country." Imagine three hundred million eyes and ears alert and aware of what's going on in our communities. Take a casserole over, throw a block party, have a welcome committee stop by—do something! Let's return to the old norm, where we knew each other and cared about our neighbors. When in doubt, call the proper authority. If you're concerned, we all should be.

When I was eleven or twelve, Mom told me to go cut Mrs. Swartz's lawn. Mrs. Swartz was an elderly woman living by herself across the street. Her husband had passed away the previous year. I asked how much she was going to pay me. Mom said, "She's not paying you anything. She's living on a fixed income and needs help. You'll do it for free and be nice." At first, I grudgingly cut the old lady's lawn. One day, a neighbor walking by asked how much I was charging Mrs. Swartz. I said wasn't charging her anything because she was old, on some kind of limited income, and could not pay me. The neighbor said I was doing a good job and that he'd pay me ten bucks to cut his lawn. By the end of the month, I had three paying customers and the best cookies ever from Mrs. Swartz. Kindness and support are always rewarded, sometimes directly and sometimes not so directly. I didn't know it then, but I know it now, and I hope those who helped me are being rewarded too.

* * *

We were there for our friends in good times and bad. One Halloween, Gary was away, so Doris, Judy, and I went to the Officer's Club Halloween Party as a shotgun wedding. I hate to admit this, but I think I came up with the idea. Doris, the husband, Judy, the much-offended father of the bride demanding honor via wedding nuptials, and I, the demur pregnant bride, veil, and all were a sight to behold. Doris and Judy wore overalls, suspenders, eye shadow mustaches, and hillbilly hats. Judy carried a fake shotgun and an appropriate scowl. I was not used to wearing a veil, and after tipping back a few, I walked right through a screen door.

Oscar-Worthy Exit

A typhoon struck our home on Guam. The rain and winds were unceasingly brutal. The wind pushed the torrential rains into the house. It was a cinder blockhouse, and water seeped in between the blocks at an alarming rate. The water level rose rapidly, especially in the bedroom. I ran to Judy's house to find her on the verge of panic. I grabbed the baby and led Judy by the arm to ride out the storm at our place. We arrived to find the water ankle deep in most rooms. The living room seemed to be the highest point in the house and the driest. We were living on Nimitz Hill, the highest point on the island, and we were damn near underwater. It didn't make sense to me. The roads were closed, travel was unwise, and there we had nowhere to go. We moved the king-size bed into the living room. Doris, Judy, and I, along with the three kids, sat on the bed, watching the water rise. We played cards, rocked the babies to sleep, and prayed the storm would soon subside. We were plotting our next moves. The water kept rising, our anxiety did as well, and it didn't look good. We were helpless.

As suddenly as it started, it stopped. We welcomed the silent void after the howling winds. Doris and Judy began bailing out the houses and trying to resume some semblance of normalcy. I went outside to assess the damage. My car, a new forest green Ambassador, from the American Motors Corp., was parked in the carport, and it had taken on water. If we wanted to escape in it, I'd need an oar. I opened the car door, and a wave of water washed over me.

Not my kind of island.

Chapter Four

THE REDHEADED STEPCHILD

Mom thought we were the Kennedys without the money.

We were a large New England Irish Catholic family. I was number two of a clan that would end up with a total of ten. Mom had ten children, her sister had ten children, and her brother had five. Twenty-five grandchildren were gifted to the grandparents from three siblings. I was not adopted, but I felt like they may have mixed up the babies at the hospital and put me with the wrong family. I always felt like the odd man out, the redheaded stepchild. I grew up before and during the Age of Aquarius, I went to sock hops, homecomings, and hayrides. I was even on the TV show *American Bandstand*.

Our family had seven boys and three girls, and Mom's sister had eight girls and two boys. The oldest two boys and two girls from each family appeared on the show hosted by Dick Clark and danced to the music of the sixties. Don't tell anyone, but the cousins arrived a day late, and we missed the real date for our dance debut. Mom forged the tickets by changing the date, and then sweet-talked our way into the show when confronted at the door. Our folks did their best, and we were loved and cared for to the best of any parent's capabilities.

When I talk about my family, it's almost as if there were two families—two sets of parents and two eras of reality. The older kids, number one through four, and the younger, five through ten, will each tell a different story. As number two of ten, this is mine.

Dad was tough. He wanted to forge men of steel, and we were governed by the old adages "Men don't cry" and "Pick yourself up by your bootstraps and carry on no matter what." Dad, stern and hard in his demeanor, believed in don't spare the rod. I once asked Dad, "Don't you want me to like you? Don't you want to be my friend?" His most revealing answer was, "I'm your parent first, and maybe we can be friends later. My job is to raise you and be your parent, not your friend." He ruled with an iron fist and disciplined with the strap, and he slipped into Alzheimer's before he became my friend.

I don't know how to define my dad in today's terms, but it wouldn't be with all kind and supportive adjectives. He tried to be a parent, and he did what he thought best, and the ten siblings didn't turn out too bad.

* * *

His discipline hurt. I stole a cookie from the cookie jar and was grounded for two weeks. I lied, and he took the belt to me. If I disobeyed or talked back, I got all the above. He was considered mean by all the extended families. Aunts and Uncles would discipline their kids by saying if you don't behave, I'm going to send you to Uncle Bill's. I wonder how I would have developed if he turned a blind eye and didn't enforce his beliefs. Is he right to say we must be parents first and friends later? Through his discipline, I learned to respect authority, and when someone says, "Hands above your head so I can see them and don't move," I comply. I learned the value of work and how to earn my own way and to show respect for others. Was it too extreme? Have we gone too far the other way? I worry what will happen if we don't discipline, if we don't coach and don't engage with our children.

I worry we lost the sense of family that I grew up with. We were required to be at the dinner table a 6:00 p.m. We talked through dinner and solved problems. We fought over who could have the car for the Friday night football game. We went to school activities as a family and supported one another.

* * *

We are defined by moments and seconds. We are lost and found in those moments. My first moment came when we lived in Rhode Island in the early 1950s. The house was deathly quiet on an ominously dark night. I looked out the window. I couldn't see beyond my little reflection in glass—unkempt brown hair with the unmanageable cowlick on the back of my head and teasing brown eyes that usually invited laughter or at least a giggle. The darkness morphed around my reflected image and consumed my attention as it seemed to become fluid. The roiling dark threat tried to slither its way under the window sash and sit with us on that quiet night. I wasn't scared.

I ripped my gaze away from the menacing shadows and walked across the room to sit beside my brother on the green and off-white floral couch. Together, we could've handled whatever the night might have threatened. I felt that connectedness that assured me we could handle anything together. I scooted a little closer to Billy on the couch just to be sure.

Dad had gone to get dinner because he didn't feel like cooking. As he was putting on his coat, he said, "You boys okay by yourself if I just run down the street and get us some dinner?" Being the grown men of six or seven he wanted us to be, we said, "Yes, Daddy," and off he went.

Mom was in the hospital having another baby. I wasn't quite sure why we needed another one. I was perfectly happy with Billy next to me and Michael in the crib down the hall. We didn't need any more kids, especially any girl kids. Mom had said something about girls. I knew that would be the worst.

The silence intensified as the wind off the ocean whistled up the street to empower the darkness that surrounded our small New England house. The house groaned. The wooden floors and the pointed roof stretched and bent until chills ran up and down my back.

Billy flipped on the TV to distract us. The snowy screen blinked and hissed white noise as it warmed up. An eerie black cross with circles around it appeared before the local station fluttered into view with pictures in shades of black and white. Billy flipped through two or three stations, the only ones we could get, and I adjusted the rabbit ears to get a better picture. We settled on a detective show.

I began to feel a bit better until the TV depicted a guy walking down the sidewalk. He was in a suit and tie like Dad wore to work, and he carried a briefcase as he moved swiftly down the street. The music was haunting, and this guy kept looking over his shoulder. Suddenly, a bandit stepped out of the alley and whacked him on the back of the head with a blackjack. The bad guy wore a narrow mask that tied behind his head and encircled his dark eyes. He looked like a 160-pound raccoon on two legs. The blackjack was curved and black and menacing. The robber snatched the briefcase out of the unconscious man's hand and raced off down the street.

I scooted even further towards Billy. He didn't seem to mind. We started at mildly jittery and worked our way into terrified in about two seconds. Billy turned off the TV, returning us to the haunting whistles of the little Cape Cod house.

"Should we check on Michael?" Billy whispered, not moving from his spot.

The baby, in the back bedroom down a long dark hallway, was quiet. The tiny two-bedroom house somehow magnified itself into a haunted mansion. I knew without a doubt that Mr. Raccoon was located somewhere between the floral couch and the crib

"I'm not going," I whispered back.

Billy frowned. "Well, I'm not going either."

The silence swelled and engulfed us, and I wondered if my father had been hit in the head like the man on the TV and our dinner stolen by Mr. Raccoon.

The situation called for a hero, and I'd always wanted and still want to be the hero. I put on my little jacket, mustered up as much courage as a six-year-old can, and ventured out into the dark, black night. I trudged across a grassy wasteland, no more than a ten-foot lawn, and knocked on the neighbor's door. Mr. Corbett answered the door, blinking down at me in surprise. The bright lights from his living room haloed his large frame and seemed to whisper warmth and safety. I knew I'd done right. I stated the purpose of my visit, asking him to come sit with us until Dad returned. With little convincing, he put on his jacket and yelled to someone that he'd be back soon. He held my hand as we walked back across the wasteland. I already felt better.

We sat in the living room, not the least concerned about Raccoon Man, and we never thought of the poor businessman again. I was damned proud. I rose to the occasion, much like a hero would. I contemplated a cape.

Then Dad came home.

I don't remember the look on his face, but the silence was deep and dreadful. I wanted to turn the TV back on and take my chances.

"Thank you for coming," Dad said before he promptly ushered Mr. Corbett out of the house. We waited, almost as afraid of him as we had been of Mr. Raccoon.

"Which one of you went after him?" he said, looming over us.

Luckily, our neighbor hadn't specified who'd trudged over to request his services. Billy, not so diplomatic, pointed at me with his thumb over his shoulder and scooted a bit to distance himself and not be tarnished by the guilty. Pushed under the bus, I could feel the tire tracks that broke the connection with big brother, and I was alone.

Still believing myself a hero, I didn't deny a thing. We were frightened, and I solved the problem and saved the day. Both of us were glad for the company.

Dad began to pace in front of me, huffing like an angry bull. His tirade dripped with sarcasm like "my big boys," "my brave sons," "my cowards," "couldn't be left alone for just a short time," "made a bad decision," "not the sons I thought I was raising," and on and on. He not only said those things that night but every time a male relative came into the house, the story was relived. He especially liked to tell his brother Joe. He would repeat the story in front of me, embellishing those adjectives that would soon define me. Coward. Failure. Unwanted.

Memories Run Permanent and Deep Sometimes

Now I had two problems. One, the food he bought home for dinner was bar food, and it had gotten cold. Number two was that I believed him. I've always thought I wasn't the son he wanted. This, overtime, translated into I'm not the brother, the friend, the boyfriend, the husband, and the employee anyone wanted.

I kept up the struggle to be the hero, to win, or to be just one of the guys. Once I was part of an apple fight with a bunch of neighbor kids, and I knew my team would be the victors. I didn't even want to throw these stupid apples at my friends, but I couldn't let on, they'd think I was a sissy. I could see the other guys in the orchard under the apple trees. They had an unlimited arsenal, and we only had what we could carry out in one armload. How was I going to be the hero and lead my team to win the battle of all apple fights? Micah was on the other team, and he's my best buddy, but I've got to win. Dad said something about having to win because there is only one first place, and all the rest are losers. We were running out of ammo, and I saw some of my teammates heading home in defeat. I needed a solution. I looked around and saw a jagged stone about the size of a golf ball, and the answer became clear.

Fueled by the need to win, to fit in, and to be one of those guys everyone wanted me to be, I hurled the stone in an arc high above the trees so it would fall through the branches and knock lose hundreds of apples on the unsuspecting enemy team. In my mind's eye, I could see my guys carrying me off the field on their shoulders as the defeated team scattered and ran home crying. I could see them come out from under the trees screaming and swatting apples away like they were running through a hoard of bees. I'd be damned if we were going to be losers, even if I already felt like one.

I waited to hear the stone thrash through the leaves. I waited to hear the apples thudding to the ground. Only silence reigned. Suddenly the quiet erupted in a heart-stopping scream, followed by the panicked snapping of the underbrush. Micah raced out of the trees with blood pouring down his face. He had one hand on his forehead as if holding it on. Blood seeped through his fingers, ran down his cheeks, over his lips and chin, and pooled on his shirt. His house was close by, and he dashed for the back door, screaming. The jagged stone hit him in the middle of his forehead.

Before he reached the stoop, his mother, recognizing the screams, flung open the back door. She raced to meet him, horrified at the sight. I can still see the look on her face. She grabbed him up, folded him in her arms, and rushed him into the house. Eerie quiet returned.

Failure, Again

There was no downpour of apples. There was no victory. I was not carried off the field of battle on anyone's shoulders. No one saw me throw the stone. No one knew what had happened or how Micah got such a gash on his face. I slinked home in shame. I wanted to fit in. I wanted to be one of the guys. I wanted to win. I wanted to be the hero. But that's not how I felt.

The scars aren't always internal, and shortly after my historic failure, I crashed and burned a second time. This time I had an audience.

As kids, we traveled in packs with or without our parents. On a beautiful Saturday morning, our pack attended First Communion practice. On the way home, as I sat by the window in the back seat of our station wagon, listening to the gang laugh, chatter, and rehash, how we were going to receive the Holy Ghost the next day. I wondered if the rest of the kids from our class in the car behind us, driven by Mrs. Kent, sounded the same. First Communion meant we were growing up and just a stone's throw from being a preteen. That analogy conjures bad memories.

Headed to First Communion practice

First Communion

I looked out the window at the trees passing rapidly by, the colors of deep yellow and red leaves blending into a kaleidoscopic blur. Mom saw me pressed against the window, and she said, "Is that door locked?"

I checked, and the door looked like it wasn't quite closed all the way. I couldn't lock the door if it wasn't closed tightly. I opened the door a bit intending to slam it completely shut and then lock it. The wind whiplashed the door violently and snapped it on its hinges to the fully open position. Not letting go of the handle, I became attached to the open door, dangling over the road below.

Stunned, startled, and terrified, I just hung there for a few seconds. With my body twisted and my side against the door, I was looking back into our car and directly into the eyes of my buddy. His eyes were opened so wide he looked like a painting by Margaret D. H. Keane of a boy watching his best buddy hang on for dear life. I lost my grip and dropped silently and painfully to the road.

I tumbled down the road toward the car behind us, feeling trapped in a slow-motion film, when in fact, it had happened in seconds. The other car barreled toward me, and the screeching of brakes from both cars drowned out my screaming. I didn't realize I had started screaming. The cars careened to a halt half on, half off the road. The screaming I heard was not mine. Both car loads of kids were screaming as they saw me come to rest against the tire of the car behind us. The mother driving the second car stopped just in time. My face, raked bloody from the wrestling match with the street, gave testament that the street obviously won.

Mom picked me up off the street and held me as she shepherded the kids from our car into the second car. She then raced to the nearest doctor's office with me in the front seat, my head on her lap. The red colors now were not those of autumn beauty; they were the color of my blood on me and Mom's blouse.

The left side of my face, embedded with pebbles, dirt, gravel, and whatever else was on the road where I landed, frightened everyone in the waiting room of the doctor's office. The doctor gave me a shot. Next thing I knew I was coming out of the anesthesia in Dad's arms. The doctor knocked me out so he could take a brush to my cheek to clean up the mess. Dad came from work to assist so Mom could get home. As Dad carried me to the car, I came in and out of a fog. I felt safe one minute and not so good the next. I heard Dad mutter, "You, chowder head." I guess that's a New England phrase for stupid. The echo of coward, failure, and being unwanted rang out dimly in the background of my fogged mind.

Did I become unlovable at that moment? I thought of it in terms of parents ordering a mail-ordered son. They are first presented with an order form where they get to select the traits they want in their new sons, soon to be shipped to them. Would they have checked the box that said, "Gets scared by the TV?" No, I don't think so. "Needs someone to hold his hand crossing the wasteland of a night-shrouded lawn, and is he afraid of the dark?" No, I don't think so. "Can't make good decisions?" No, not really. "Is weak and cowardly like the lion in *The Wizard of Oz*?" I don't think so.

We were not aware of other boxes they might have checked, but the answer to these would have been a definite no. Believing I was not what my father wanted haunted me most of my life. I spent the better part of my life trying to prove I was smart enough, fast enough, strong enough, and handsome enough to be a son, or brother, or friend. I worked hard to be courageous, strong, and worthy of love. I worked hard to be a person I could love.

Another defining moment came when Dad nicknamed me. I visualize him sitting in his wingback chair with a loud floral pattern that didn't match the couch. He always sat there. The floor lamp standing between his chair and the window filtered light through the old plastic-covered shade and cast a halo effect around him. He was waiting for the paperboy to deliver the evening newspaper—waiting impatiently. The newspaper, delivered by a kid from the neighborhood, finally landed on the front stoop with a dull thud. The delivery boy raced down the sidewalk on his bike, tossing the papers over his head, hoping to land them somewhere near the front doors of each subscriber's home. Most of the time, he was successful. Sometimes we had to pick the paper out the hedge or the weeds or, on a really bad day, from the neighbor's yard.

I was on the floor watching TV, and Dad said, "Crisco, you hear that? Go get the newspaper." The tone didn't illicit admiration or love. My brothers snickered.

Without any visible reaction that I was aware of, I got up and headed for the front door. I wondered if I should bark like a dog on my way out. Nicknames weren't unusual in our house. Jock, Stud, Joey, Billy…any one of those would have been just fine, but he called me "Crisco." He had called me that for a while, and I don't know whether I just didn't understand what he was saying, or I just didn't want to know where the name came from. Dad's words could sting.

I walked very slowly to the front door and picked up the paper. I stalled some more on my return trip, wanting to confront him but dreading the exchange. He yelled something about taking too long, so I picked up the pace and returned to the den. I handed him his paper. He opened it ceremoniously and began muttering. His elbows rested on the arms of the chair, and he held the paper up crisply in front of his face.

I stood in front of him, not sure if I wanted a thank you or an explanation. Enough was enough.

"Why do you call me Crisco?" I said to the paper.

A loud, crumpling sound followed as he crushed the paper into his lap. He sighed and scowled. He didn't like to be disturbed when he was reading the paper.

He said, "What is Crisco?"

I said, "That stuff Mom uses to grease the pans when she's cooking."

He responded with, "Gooooood. That's right. Fat in the can like you."

Fat in the can be translated as "I had a lard ass or fat ass." Good to know.

I tried to look over my shoulder to verify that fact but couldn't see the offending "can." The newspaper, now crushed and wrinkled, came back up in front of his face in a dismissive flourish. For some time, I imagined a bulbous butt trailing behind me, leaving ruts in the sidewalk.

Reality is I have a nice butt admired by many and envied by a few, but the power of the message transformed reality. I became the mocking phrases of Dad and others who chose to bully me.

Regardless of his style, he was always my father, and his style made me seek strength and courage. His letters to me while I was in Nam depicted another side of the man I called Dad. He didn't know how to verbalize feelings and his vision for his children. He didn't have a role model for parenting. He just disciplined, demanded, and in some cases, demeaned. His letters, to the contrary, depicted a thoughtful and caring parental nature. It was confusing, but I never felt he wasn't trying to do his best. I wondered, "Was he mean or thoughtful? Did he care, or was it something else?" Did he write letters to Vietnam because he thought I wasn't coming back, just as Mom's similar fear motivated the family the photo? It doesn't matter now. His advice was valuable, and I choose to believe he cared. His style gave me great negotiating skills and stamina. I did what I thought was right then, and I laughed and cried to my own life's music. I wanted to be on Broadway and be the leading man; I wanted to be the star, the hero.

Wrapping up my training in early 1968, I flew many missions, six-hour missions, ten-hour missions, even though I had a fear of flying that I couldn't acknowledge or verbalize. I wrote my father a letter saying I wanted to change my billet. I wanted a job that did not include flying. I wasn't going to ask to avoid Vietnam, just not fly. My father wrote,

> Joe, it is a brave and wise man that recognizes fear, admits its existence and then trys to work out a plan to accomplish what he has set out to do in spite of this fear. If your only reason for wanting to change your program is a fear of flying then I say do *not* change. Stay in, combat the fear, and overcome it. Fear of flying, today, is like being afraid of the automobile 50 years ago. It is inconceivable to us, now, that people used to feel automobiles went too fast, were liable to blow-up and in general were just something for dare devils to kill themselves in. Keep in mind the fact that their fears were not completely unjustified many people were and still are killed violently in automobiles, but can you imagine getting along in today's world if you wouldn't ride in an automobile? In your lifetime the airplane will be as important to enjoying life and conducting your business properly as the auto-

mobile is now. You don't want to be like the Amish people in Morgantown, still in a horse and wagon, because of a fear that I'm sure you are man enough to face and conquer.

If it's just that you don't like flying and would prefer some other type of duty, then by all means change, and change quickly as possible. If you are to do your job well you must be happy with your work. The services don't always allow you complete freedom of choice, but to the extent you have it exercise this choice and get into a field that appeals to you and that you feel that you can do well in.

The decision is yours, Joe, and I know you'll make a sound one. One thing Mom said, was that you could get out in 3 instead of 4 years if you got out of flight training. If this is so, and you don't think you will make a career of the Navy then this is the most important reason to change. The sooner you can get your tour over and get out the better it is if you don't plan to stay with it for 20 or 30 years...

2-13-68

Dear Joe,

Your letter pleased me very much. It's gratifying to have anyone turn to you for advice, but especially so when it is someone who for many years got advice from you whether he wanted it or not. Finding that you're not "fed up" with advice from me gives me a very warm feeling.

Joe, it's a brave and wise man that recognizes fear, admits its existence, and then tries to work out a plan to accomplish what he has set out to do in spite of this fear. If your only reason for wanting to change your program is a fear of flying then I say do not change. Stay in, combat the fear, and overcome it. Fear of flying, today, is like being afraid of the automobile 50 years ago. It is inconceivable to us, now, that people used to feel automobiles went too fast, were liable to blow up and in general were just something for dare-devils to kill themselves in. Keep in mind the fact that their fears were not completely unjustified, many people were and still are killed violently in automobiles, but can you imagine getting along in today's world if you wouldn't ride in an automobile? In your lifetime the airplane will be as important to enjoying life and conducting your business properly as the automobile is now. You don't want to be like the Amish people in Morgantown, still in a horse and wagon, because of a fear that I'm sure you are man enough to

Letter to Vietnam

If it's just that you don't like flying and would prefer some other type of duty, then by all means change, and change as quickly as possible. If you are to do your job well you must be happy with your work. The services don't always allow you complete freedom of choice, but to the extent that you have it exercise this choice and get into a field that appeals to you and that you feel that you can do well in.

The decision is yours, Joe, and I know you'll make a sound one. One thing you didn't mention in your letter, that I think Mom said, was that you could get out in 3 instead of 4 years if you got out of flight training. If this is so, and you don't think you will make a career of the Navy then this is the most important reason to change. The sooner you can get your tour over and get out the better it is if you don't plan to stay with it for 20 or 30 years.

Let me think a little longer on the question of a gift for Dor.

Please don't even think of sending us money until you are on even keel, have all the uniforms you need, finish your payments in Ea. Lansing and are sure that what you send isn't needed for your day to day expenses. We have no problems that we can't handle.

On the question of the books and Rossi, I would drop him a line and explain the situation. Suggest that you send the book to him complete, and someone at the bank can remove one at the end of each month. If this isn't OK. he will then

Letter to Vietnam (cont.)

Forty-five years later, in January 2013, I landed a contract in Chicago that had me commuting every week from San Diego to Chicago. It was lucrative and challenging, and I'm not sure I would have been able to do it if I hadn't overcome or mollified some of those fears of flying.

* * *

Many of our Navy pilots were superb. Skip, my aircraft commander, was a great example, and we flew many missions together. I confided in him about my fear of flying. He took me under his wing, literally, and confidently decided to show me how safe it was to fly. Really. We were taking off from the Philippines headed to Da Nang. Skip said, "I want you to come up to the cockpit and stand behind me for this flight." Now I had never gone to the cockpit because I didn't want to see all that open sky I could fall from. Nine thousand feet is a lot of feet, and I never mastered the theory of heavier than air flight. In fact, I wish the Wright Brothers had invented vacuum cleaners instead.

I stood behind the pilot's seat, unbuckled, unnerved, and looked at that blue sky with its billowing white cotton clouds and saw my life flash before my eyes as I was sure the end was near, and we were still on the ground. Skip rolled the plane out, lined up on the numbers at the end of the runway, went BTW (balls to the wall), meaning full throttle, and we headed down the runway.

Takeoffs were never smooth. Howard Hughes designed the original Constellation aircraft in the 1930s, and we called the ones we flew fifty thousand bolts in loose formation. The old big plane lumbered down the runway. It did not glide or sail. I was convinced liftoff was but a dream. Soon, but not soon enough for me, the nose came up, and the beast, the second

97

beast in my life, went airborne, banking to the right onto our assigned flight path.

I was waiting for Skip to level out and fly straight. I didn't like this banking thing or any banking maneuver. He never leveled off.

I hear, "Mayday, Mayday." I knew Skip wasn't announcing a dance. I saw sweat pouring out of the back of his hairline, down his neck, and into his flight suit. It looked like a mini-Niagara Falls less than a foot in front of me. All human functions I own ceased, and I knew all my fears were well founded. Skip kept the plane in a right bank, flying around the tower, and right back down onto the runway we just left. Smooth as silk. After that, I had to excuse myself and change my silks.

It's a miracle I ever flew again. I don't know all the technical flight jargon for what went mechanically wrong, but I know we were on the ground for almost a full week waiting for a replacement whatchamacallit to be flown in to repair the aircraft. It was a part that apparently didn't need replacing very often because the old part we pulled out the plane was dated 1935.

Later, I said to Skip, "You were really worried about that problem, weren't you?"

He said, "Oh, no. I had it under control."

I asked, "Then why were you sweating so badly and so tense?"

Skip clarified that he was sweating about the possibility that something else might go wrong. "I had this situation under control, but if one more thing went wrong, I could not have handled it," he said. "We had no additional resources or options left. I used them all up to get us back on the ground safely."

I later related to this experience. In Vietnam, I had used up all my love, courage, and strength. I had that situation under control, but if one more thing went wrong, could I handled it?

Did I have resources left to handle the next battle? Since we live life on life's terms, eventually one more thing did go wrong.

I thought if I told about my fears and failures, I'd be living up to that prevailing feeling that I was not enough, and I was not the person anyone wanted. I had trouble replacing that feeling with the knowledge and awareness to be human. I fear, occasionally fail, hurt, laugh, and love, and sometimes not in the right order, and that's the beauty of me. Joy is hard to come by, happiness is elusive, and the journey becomes weary.

* * *

The lazy hot Pennsylvania summer of 1962 had come to an end. School opened that September and I became a high school senior. Seniors were BMOC. Big men on campus knew what to do, how to act, and could handle anything. If only that were true.

The first week of school, I visited with the English teacher who doubled as the director for the high school's plays. I asked what shows he had picked for the year. He said in the spring they were doing *The Many Loves of Dobie Gillis*, and he hoped I'd audition. He thought I'd make a good Dobie. It wasn't every day that someone had faith in me to do well. It wasn't every day someone was inviting me to be a part of things instead of insisting I sit down or just leave.

I rushed home and announced to everyone present that I planned to try out for the lead in the senior play. I felt there was a chance I'd get it. There were murmurs of excitement and jealousy from my siblings. Mom opened her mouth to say something, but a resounding "No, you're not" interrupted her.

It came from the wingback chair. Stunned into momentary silence, I stood still as a statue. I knew this role would be the highlight of my senior year, maybe even my life. I began babbling nonstop. I told Dad about my talk with the director. I assured him the school needed me to do this, and the director asked me to try out—on and on. We negotiated on and off, mostly off, for the rest of the late afternoon and early evening. I eventually resorted to begging, but he held fast. The knots in my stomach prevented me from eating. Mom, obviously in my corner, gave me looks that showed she understood. She tried to get me to relax and eat, but she never said a word to Dad. Mom didn't cross Dad. I wasn't sure if she saw her role as the biblical, obedient wife, or if she simply didn't want to pick a fight.

After much begging, pleading, and probably some tears, I don't want to admit to because BMOC don't cry, the compromise was uttered from on high. The terms were as follows: I could try out for the spring play if I engaged in a sport in the fall. Men played sports, not a role in the school play. Dad, recognizing that I did not have a natural desire to play sports, decided he needed to force the issue.

According to Dad, participating in sports made you a man. I wasn't sure what going out for the play labeled me. Sports never ranked high with me. I didn't fit the profile. I was not graceful and fluid. I was not built like a brick shit house, and I injured myself often. I did track and field my junior year. I ran the hurdles, the low ones. I was taught to sail over the wooden barriers with one leg perpendicular to the ground in front of me and the other similarly stretched out behind. When I watched someone else do it, they looked like poetry in motion. I would come out of the chocks racing furiously and sail over the first hurdle in semifine form, but by the second or third leap, I was convinced the hurdles were getting higher. I knew what would happen, and sure enough, one of those stupid wood crossbeams hit me in the most sensitive of areas. I couldn't quit because that would make me a failure, so I just kept going on and on.

When Dad tossed that compromise into the conversation, I immediately agreed. I would do anything. Well, not *anything* because I wasn't going over those hurdles again. But I would try out for the football team.

Autumn was arriving, the warm summer days became history, and football season was upon us. The first meeting to select potentials player started late in the day, after school. I sat in the bleachers with about twenty to thirty other kids. We all waited apprehensively, hoping to be selected for the prestigious honor of being on the high school football team. The girls all loved the football jocks, and while I didn't try out for that reason, it wasn't a bad incentive. Look good at all costs.

Sitting there, I flashed back to all the pickup games my brothers and I had played, whether baseball, football, hide-and-seek, or anything. Most of the guys were picked long before anyone considered me. The teams argued about who had to pick me, not who wanted me. Each team captain tried to pawn me off to the other team so they would have a leg up and potentially win. But that was then, and this was now, and I was going to make the team and show them all.

The coach went person to person, asking some basic questions, and getting to know each one of us. He had gray hair peeking out from under a ball cap, wire-rimmed glasses, a huge red nose, and he carried a clipboard. He kept referring to the clipboard as if it was the Bible, and he jotted notes about the prospective players and their responses. He came to me and asked what position I wanted to play. I excitedly responded, "I want to be a thrower." The silence was frightening. The look on the coach's face reminded me of Dad when he came home and saw Mr. Corbett sitting in the living room with us.

The silence ended as the coach flung his hands up into the air and lost his grip on his clipboard. The clipboard went sailing over his head, scattering papers everywhere. He glared at me like

101

I just broke wind. My classmates were stunned into silence and concern. I apparently just committed a felony. Coach raised his right arm, bent at the elbow with his thumb, pointing over his right shoulder toward the gate, and said, "Get out. Now. I need passers, not throwers. I've got plenty of throwers." I was unceremoniously thrown out of tryouts without touching pigskin. Failure. My peers' silence made me feel as alone and humiliated as I had ever been.

When I got home, Dad sitting in his damn chair again, asked how the tryouts went. I hung my head and admitted not so good. I recounted the story and watched Dad's head turning left and right in continuous disapproval. All he said was, "You better keep trying or no Dobie."

So I joined the wrestling squad with my brother. I wrestled with my weight and with opponents week after week, hating most of it. It didn't help with my weight that Mrs. Derstine, the Pennsylvania Dutch cook who helped Mom, came each week and baked chocolate chip cookies, apple pies, and apple coffee cakes and other goodies. I ate my share and then stole a few more pieces or a few more cookies every Thursday. When we weighed in for the Saturday wrestling match, I saw the scale settle three to four pounds over the limit. Hours had to be spent in the sauna, in sweat gear doing jumping jacks to get the weight down. Not my thing. I wanted to go back to the kitchen, the cookies, and the pies, but I did like the camaraderie of the team. The male bonding, the closeness of my teammates, and the accolades when I won. Still, it was not my thing. I had a strong sense of attraction to the sport that I couldn't explain, but overall, being thrown around or knocking someone else down and trying to bend them like a pretzel didn't thrill me.

I wrestled my way to second place in the state of Pennsylvania in the 136-pound weight class. I probably could have gotten the ribbon for first place, but I was looking around to see if Dad was watching and cheering me on, like I always did. He wasn't, and I got pinned by my opponent. No big deal. Mine is not a story of *I can't*. It's a story of *that's not me*. Unfortunately, for years, I believed that *I couldn't* because I was not good enough, not smart enough, not strong enough, and not the son Dad wanted.

I collected my ribbon for second place and headed home. Dad was in his chair, watching a football game on TV. I walked over and handed him the ribbon. He looked at it and figured I just wanted a compliment. He said, "Nice." Then he reached out to give the ribbon back to me.

I didn't move to take it back. A bit irritated, he said, "Take your ribbon and put it upstairs on your dresser next to Billy's." Billy's ribbon was for first place in his weight class. I still didn't move to take the ribbon back. I just stared at him, and he stared back with a look that would make a parrot fall off its perch. He got very upset and thrust the ribbon toward me, saying, "Take it. It's yours."

I said, "No, it's not. It's yours. I never wanted it."

He never understood, and he certainly never asked.

When the cold winter began to thaw, my excitement bloomed. The spring semester of my senior year roared nearer and nearer. I thanked the stars above that wrestling season was over. I'd kept my part of the bargain. I put *x*'s on the calendar for all the days between then and the auditions for the spring play. I sat in the auditorium and dreamed of the crowds leaping to their feet as I entered stage right.

The big day came, and I stood on an empty stage, reading lines for the role of Dobie Gillis. There was no outside world at that moment. It was just me, as Dobie, and the eyes of onlookers watching and measuring. Three of us vied for the part. The other guys were bigger, more popular, and more handsome. I sat and watched them and worried. They were good. So far, all life's lessons had taught me, I measured just shy of good enough.

The decisions on who got selected for the cast and what role they were going to play would be posted on a bulletin board within the week. The list would be available when we arrived at school. I couldn't sit still. I woke up in the middle of the night to thunderous applause and asked Mom a million times if she thought I'd get the part. The morning the list was supposed to be posted, I almost didn't want to go to school. I got off the bus and lingered outside the old brick building, afraid. Even if Dad didn't want me to be in the play, I didn't want to fail because I wanted it like nothing I'd ever wanted before.

I heard the white double doors burst open and bang against the metal railings. I looked up to see Sue, who tried out for the lead female role, busting out of the building. She saw me, and she yelled, "Hey, Dobie!"

I had done it. I had landed the lead role. This was my ribbon. I couldn't have been happier. Maybe being sort of awkward and ungainly paid off. I was finally part of something. I fit into the role and the cast of Dobie Gillis. I just wanted to be me and connected to something. I practiced for hours after school and at home in front of the mirror. I tried different sounding voices and reached inflections I didn't know existed in me. I tried on different sweaters and shoes. I combed my hair differently every night. I was going to be a star, the star.

Dobie Gillis and costar

The cast stood or sat in position on pins and needles as the curtain went up opening night. We played to a full house that Friday night and closed the next night to a standing ovation. Dad showed up Saturday evening with Mom. He wasn't impressed, and he said nothing. I think Mom forced him to go. I was elated. Nothing was going to spoil this for me, not even him.

The director took the cast out to dinner at a fancy restaurant in Philadelphia to celebrate a job well done. As we ate, laughed, and relived the Dobie moments, regaling in our success, one cast member said, "Hey, isn't that Peter and Paul of the famous singing trio Peter, Paul, and Mary?" They sat just yards from us.

Everyone leaned toward the male duo and gawked. If we were on a boat, we would have capsized. Everyone agreed the two guys really were the singers. We debated whether it would be okay to go over and say hello. I'm not sure there was any consensus or agreement, but as if on cue, the cast bolted over to their table asking for their autographs.

I, a star in my own right, did not race over in such a pedestrian fashion begging for their autograph. Instead, I sat alone on my side of the restaurant with my star-studded nose high in the air. One of the two, Peter or Paul, asked our troupe who they were. "We are the cast of Dobie Gillis," they excitedly relayed. One of the singers asked who played the role of Dobie. They pointed in my direction.

Completely aware they were talking about me, I gave them a regal wave. Peter and Paul conspiratorially whispered with my castmates. I waited as two very excited peers raced back to my table. "Peter and Paul want to know if you'd give them your autograph," they said.

Without a moment's hesitation, I moved my Coke off my soggy cocktail napkin, signed my name, and waltzed across the restaurant. I presented Peter and Paul with my John Hancock as if it was the norm of my paparazzi-chased life. We engaged in idle chitchat for a brief period, and then I returned to my dinner. If I could have lived off that high forever, my life would have been entirely different.

I arrived home late that Saturday evening. I let myself in the back door. The quiet house felt lonely, and I was greeted by a dim night-light illuminating the kitchen. I saw a huge bouquet of roses on the kitchen table. I tore open the card, addressed to me, and saw they were from the ladies I worked with at the pill-packing factory. The ladies came to my rescue again. They tried but had not been allowed to give me the roses onstage. The school didn't want to show favoritism.

Dad did not buy the roses, nor was he waiting up to congratulate me on my success. The roses should have been a reminder that I was loved and supported. Instead, I was reminded that I wasn't quite good enough. I wasn't what Dad had in mind.

* * *

Dad had this rule not to swear in front of Mother. I don't know why because when Mom got pissed at Dad, she would give him the middle finger. It was the subtle, delicate New England finger where she raised her right hand, middle finger extended, and gently pressed the bridge of her glasses against her nose as if adjusting the perfectly positioned glasses. It was the look above the glasses that let you know she was not happy.

When I was younger, I'd heard this joke in school, and I thought telling my parents a slightly "off-color" joke would make me more of an adult. As Mom sat in the passenger seat, and Dad drove, I leaned over the bench seat and boldly asked, "What happens to Confucius when he eats jelly beans?"

Both parents were stumped, and they said they didn't know.

I giggled and responded, "He shits Technicolor."

Dad attempted to regain control of the vehicle and the situation. The car swerved left and right as Dad wrestled the car back into our lane. I was thrown to the floor of the back seat by the careening automobile, but I was laughing hysterically. Dad said, "Young man, we do not swear in front of your Mother."

Mom's right hand was not adjusting her glasses. Instead, it was held against her teeth in an attempt not to laugh. Having created this awkward situation, I opted not to ask what happens to Confucius when he flies his plane upside down. He has a *crack* up. Now crack back in those days was not considered a swear word, and it wasn't an addictive substance, but I, ever so wiser, decided to keep that one to myself. It was a different time.

Early on a snowy January evening, we were all sitting around the den, each doing our thing. "Our thing" included watching TV, writing with a pen, or coloring with crayons. Technology wasn't on the horizon. Mom had delivered sibling number ten a few weeks earlier, but all was quiet. I had recently broken up with my girlfriend, and I was moping around the house. I really didn't care that we broke up. I just thought that's how people were supposed to act. I can't even remember who dumped who.

Dad sat in his chair, reading the news, talking, and barking orders from behind the paper as usual. Suddenly, he crunched the paper in his lap and said, "Jane, it's your birthday. What do you want to do to celebrate?"

Mom paused as she walked through the den and responded, "Let's take Joe bowling."

Dad reminded Mom that the doctor had told her to take it easy. Bowling could be a problem for her. The birth of her tenth child in 1962 was very difficult, and the long recovery process was not over.

Mom didn't relent. "I want to take Joe out. He's been stuck in the house helping me with the new baby. He broke up with his girlfriend, and he needs cheering up."

I was happy being inside helping with the newborn. But I didn't say anything. "You guys can bowl, and I'll keep score," she insisted. We got in the car and headed out on our winter birthday adventure.

We Didn't Get Far

A blizzard had piled snow and ice on the roadways. The billowing snow blinded us as we tried to make our way to the bowling alley. A road near our home had been narrowed to one lane, and we slowly threaded our way through the tight passage. Suddenly, bright lights loomed directly in front of us. The gleam of the oncoming headlights reflected off the snow and distorted our vision. We sat up straight in our seats and tensed as Dad stomped on the brakes. Our car swerved and went sideways up a steep snowbank. I knew we were in trouble when our headlight beams were no longer side by side but stacked vertically one on top of the other for a brief second before we slid back onto the one-lane road. The lights in front of us swerved left and right, looking like the spotlights at a grand opening. Then they settled and came straight at us.

The head-on collision sounded like a bomb going off. The event, again, transpired as if in slow motion. Metal slammed into metal, a sound like cymbals clashing. Glass cracked and shattered into a million pieces. The cascading glass made melodic sounds as the shards bounced off the hood and the door and dropped to the icy pavement. We weren't wearing seat belts. Mom was in the front passenger seat, and I sat behind her. The collision catapulted me off the seat onto the floor, wedging my legs under the front seat. Mom lurched forward, her head connecting with the windshield with a sickening crunch.

Dad yelled something. Mom screamed. Then there was nothing but silence. I feared the silence more than the scream. Silence was always the ominous warning of worse to come.

In a few moments, the slow-motion sequence ended, and the action picked up. Mom bounced back from the windshield with her head coming to rest on the top of the front seat over me. She was holding her forehead. Blood seeped through her fingers and onto me trapped in the back seat—just like Micah's head, only worse.

Dad swung open his door, leaped out, and yelled at the occupants of the other car, two teenage boys. Leaning back into our car, he glanced over the seat. "You okay?"

_id "yes" because he didn't want any other answer. Maybe I just nodded. He then grabbed Mom and dragged her out the driver's door because the car ended up wedged against a snowdrift on the right.

Luckily, a neighbor had been right behind us. The neighbor had taken his car up the snowdrift to avoid hitting us from behind. His car came to rest perpendicular to ours. Together, Dad and the neighbor hustled Mom into his car and headed to the nearest doctor's office. I was left wedged under the seat.

Emergency vehicles were not able to respond quickly. Silence resumed, only broken by the whistling wind racing through the broken windows and open doors.

I sat in the car, trapped. The cold, the loneliness, and the terror set in. I was freezing, and I couldn't move.

When an officer of the law finally arrived at the scene, he approached the accident in the same direction as the vehicle that hit us. His squad car could not pass the impact point, as both disabled vehicles were completely blocking the road. The officer removed both teenagers from their vehicle and placed them in his squad car, where he took their statements. After some time passed, he decided to walk around the scene. He was trying to corroborate what the teens told him. He duckwalked around the car to keep from slipping on the icy pavement and surveyed the damage. I saw him pass by my window. What I really saw was his big earmuffs, his warm gloves, and that big comfy coat with the fur collar. My teeth were chattering, my knees were knocking, and the rest of me was numb.

Ever so politely, I said, "Officer, could you please help me?"

I think if it hadn't been for the cold, he might've had a heart attack. He clutched at the lapel of his warm jacket, stuttered, stammered, and looked like he had just seen a ghost. He profusely apologized, extricated me from the back seat, and assisted me back to the patrol car. He needed to assist me as my legs were not working. Sitting with the two boys who had done this was difficult. Anger and silence prevailed, but I felt better in the warm car.

Numb from more than the cold and in a dreamlike state, no emotions, especially anger, were expressed. No tears, just a total disconnect from the scene. After someone picked up the other two kids, the cop drove me to the doctor's office where they were operating on Mom.

I walked into the clinic and saw nothing but the rust-red hue of blood. Instinctively, I disconnected further, retreating deeper inside myself. Mom was on an operating table and talking in a voice I did not recognize. Dad was standing next to her, holding her hand with a look I had never seen on him. He looked afraid. It had to be a bad dream. But it wasn't, and it was my fault.

Our local town doctor's office had been transformed into an operating room. The doctor's wife quickly ushered me out of the exam room and into their attached home. The woman and her son tried to cheer me up, but the effort was met with abject silence. Where did I learn silence was better than truth, and when did silence become a weapon? I used silence to intimidate, to hurt, and as an escape. Why was expressing my feelings bad, even if that included *it's my fault*, or whatever was in my heart at the time? Silence may have come from not being who or what Dad wanted me to be. If I responded, it would be the wrong response. Whatever rolled off my tongue would be wrong or stupid and just add fuel to the fire. I was surely not going to add fuel to a fire that was already ablaze.

The belief that moping around and acting all butt hurt caused us to be out in the storm became cemented in my core. Who would go out in a blizzard? If I hadn't been acting like a lost puppy, my mother would never have suggested going bowling, and she would've been home, warm and safe.

Mom had two major cuts from the broken glass. One across the width of her forehead horizontally and one vertical cut the length of her forehead right down to her eye. The vertical cut was so close to eye it cut a tear sack, and she involuntarily cried for a week. What sort of kid did that to his mother? Failure. Coward. Unwanted.

Mom was bedridden for a few days, and every time I walked into the bedroom, I burst into tears from the guilt. Mrs. Derstine had come to help during this convalescent period, and she did not approve of me being so negative. When she'd had enough of it, she snatched me up by the front of my shirt and said, "Stop crying. Your job is to cheer her up, and if you can't do that, don't go in there."

Failure. Coward. Unwanted. Shut down, Shut Out, Shut Up

Silence. I disconnected. I didn't deal with the guilt. I didn't want anyone to see my weakness. I just kept my head down and hoped that I didn't screw anything else up.

We had a thing about faces. Mom put hers through a windshield. I kissed the pavement with mine. And it didn't seem to end.

* * *

We all like to get together for reunions. We just don't talk about the white elephants sitting in the middle of the living room. We had a herd in our living room, and like any good dysfunctional family, we walked around them. We did not speak about any accidents because every time we did, Mom started crying. We didn't speak about Aunt Irene and Uncle Joe either. They drank too much. Their elephants were enormous, but we acted like it was part of the decor. Ask what's up with the elephants, the automatic curt response was, "What elephants?"

I don't remember much about Aunt Irene, just the whispers and rumors. She was on Mom's side of the family, and she was tall (at least to a ten-year-old). She had dark, unkempt hair, and the sounds I associated with her were the tinkling of ice cubes in a glass. She got "tipsy" at the reception in Narragansett Point after the painful viewing and funeral of Mom's dad.

Narragansett is a very beautiful small coastal community. The population of this narrow strip of land on the Rhode Island coast doubles during the summer months. My family was enjoying lunch and continuing the Irish wake atmosphere that felt like a party. We were at the vacation beach house of the relatives who owned the funeral home where the services were performed. Irene, unsteadily, began maneuvering herself outside when she missed a porch step and tumbled ungracefully on the sandy lawn. Her black dress waved in the breeze above her head. Her hair was in disarray. One black high heel remained on her foot, and the other was standing upright in the sand like a lawn ornament. Importantly, she didn't spill a drop of her drink, and she wasn't hurt. We breathed a sigh of relief until she decided to sue. The alcoholic must blame someone or something else. The steps caused her to fall. The steps were uneven, the steps were too narrow, or the wind. It didn't matter, just so it wasn't her.

On my father's side, Uncle Joe, dad's brother and my namesake was the white elephant. He too drank a bit. A bit is defined as a vat a day. But we didn't talk about that either.

Grandma Josephine and I spent some time together. We all called her Nana. She was the mother of Uncle Joe. The fact that Uncle Joe and I were cut from the same cloth may have made it easier for her to bond with me. Once before the ink had dried on my new driver's license, she handed me the keys to her car and said let's go. She jumped in the passenger seat, and I, behind the wheel as nervous as a wet hen approaching an electrified fence, headed off to who knows where. I'd fallen out of a moving vehicle, been in a major accident and a few minor ones. What do you expect from me, Dad? Allow me to be a little nervous.

We were running errands, I think, and she was just gabbing away, not a care in the world. Suddenly an oncoming car decided to pass a slower moving vehicle. The car moved into my lane headed directly for me. I did the only responsible thing, I panicked.

I'm sure the driver had plenty of time to overtake the car he was passing and get back in his lane, but I didn't wait to find out. I swerved right between two parked cars, wheeled around a fire hydrant, and came to a screeching stop half on and half off the sidewalk. Thank God there were no pedestrians on the sidewalk or at least my half of the sidewalk. I'd like to say this was a strategic maneuver to avoid a wreck, but it was just tactical panic on my part.

Josephine did not break into a sweat like me. She did not stop talking. She did leap out of the passenger door, race around the car, open the driver's door, and say, "Move over, Jody." For some reason, her loving nickname for me was Jody. It felt special, and I felt loved, and it was far better than other things I'd been called. She dove in, slammed the car into gear, and drove off the sidewalk like we were exiting a grocery store parking lot. She muttered, "Don't want the coppers to see us sitting on the sidewalk." Not a word about my driving, my nerves, or my character. It was just all in a day's work. Glad Dad wasn't there.

Nana's stories went on for years. One weekend, I hitchhiked home to Pennsylvania from college in Michigan. Mom and Dad were away, and Josephine had guard duty over the rest of the kids. We both were surprised to see each other. She jumped up out of her rocking chair, which sat just one foot from the TV, so she didn't miss anything, grabbed me in a bear hug, and said, "My Jody's home."

Nana then rushed out the door and down the street, hot-footing it to the liquor store to buy a six-pack of beer. We spent the rest of the evening in front of the TV. She told me the career history, life story, the scandal and gossip, and in some cases, the future of everyone on the small screen. She loved me, and she died while I served in Vietnam. She wasn't there to welcome me home and call me Jody anymore.

* * *

I should have known I'd be just like Uncle Joe and have a problem with alcohol. One of my telltale signs was my first drink. Being an awkward teenager who didn't fit in, didn't think he looked good, and didn't think he measured up didn't help. After all, I had a big butt and a face that had been dragged across a street. I had trouble asking girls out, and when I did get a date or when friends included me in any social circle, I was sullen and withdrawn. I enjoyed structured get-togethers and could be very charming with rules. I was good at following rules.

I took ballroom dance lessons at the country club, and that had a lot of structure. The girls were on one side of the room and boys on the other. When the music began, we were to walk gentlemanly-like across the room and properly ask a young lady if she wished to dance. We followed the rules for the most part. We just didn't walk; we ran across the room to get to the cute girls first. I always wanted to dance with Ruth. If I could get there first, she wouldn't say no. No threat, no harm, and no foul. I had fun with that, but take away the rules, and I was screwed.

During the summer of 1960, brother Billy, sixteen, and I, fifteen, were on a double date. I don't even remember who we were with on this infamous outing. Billy drove with his date beside him in the front seat. I, in the back seat with my date, couldn't have been more uncomfortable even if I had been sitting on a bed of coals. We were headed to an old abandoned quarry near our home in Pennsylvania. The quarry, an infamous swimming hole, became the "in" summer place for kids to hang out. We swam, necked, laughed, showed off, and had a ball. Billy's six-pack of beer helped me to have a ball. He asked if I wanted one. Being cool and grown-up, I said yeah. I drank the beer. It tasted awful, but the instantaneous and complete transformation of me can only be described as sensational.

I don't remember the names of people, brand names, time, or much of anything afterward, but I remember the feeling. It became the antidote for awkward. It provided the warmth and comfort I'd been searching for, and it became the solution. I morphed into the life of the party. I cracked jokes, talked a blue streak, and ran to join in the festivities with others. No thoughts of the negative image of me or my inadequacies existed. Rules and structure went over the cliff. I probably even flashed my fat butt, daring anyone to say anything. It felt like going from black-and-white TV to color. I had arrived. I didn't stop drinking for the next fifteen to sixteen years.

Welcome to the Fabulous Me

The lesson should have been this is not good. Having a complete psychic personality change after a drink was abnormal. Normal drinkers do not routinely have this type of change when they take a drink. Normal drinkers do not have to drink to be social. My drinking usually started before events. It's not called social drinking if a drink or two was necessary to brace up or get the courage to be social. A normal drinker, if asked, when they had their first drink will respond, I don't know maybe when I was in high school or college or who knows. I know the date, the time, the place; I know how I felt before and how I felt after; I know the details of that moment like it was etched in my brain. If you ask a normal drinker how they felt after the first drink, they may say, "Oh, I don't know. Maybe a little dizzy. Maybe a little out of control, and I didn't like it." What's not to like? That's my goal. I wanted to be out of control or at least unshackled from my awkwardness and discomfort.

Contradicting reality, I felt down, depressed, and not confident before drinking alcohol, and my solution was to imbibe a depressant and instantly get elated. Alcohol is a depressant. My mood is elevated, and I was off the charts and rocking to a new beat. That's not the normal reaction for the use of a depressant. I loved it, and I took my newfound friend with me to Vietnam.

* * *

After I left, two things went missing from my life. One was the sense of a safe community. We used to keep our doors unlocked. We knew our neighbors, and we grew up as part of a community. Beginning with the assassination of John F. Kennedy, we ceased to trust. Our world changed, and not for the better.

We locked our doors, we stopped baking casseroles, and we stopped having the neighbors over for cards. I was hitchhiking home from college the weekend JFK was assassinated, and the world stopped in shock. I got home, and for three days, I only saw the back of my mother's head as she sat, like Josephine, one foot from the TV, watching every heart-wrenching moment of our world changing. She cried and cried. She cried for JFK. She cried for Jacqueline and the kids, and when John Jr. saluted the casket, we all wept. We've lost a sense of family and community.

It had seemed so simple, so warm, and so safe, and now it felt cold, lonely, and harsh.

The second thing I missed was that innocent kid, that spunky child that put on his coat and went next door for help. I can see him as he slipped his arms in the tiny coat, walked through the kitchen, and out to head for help. I see him as he stepped out of the kitchen into a night as black as pitch.

It felt lonely and scary, but the brave little boy marched down the two or three steps, turned right, and headed for the neighbor's house. Fear flowed and ebbed like a tide on the shore. Fear washed over him, and the little boy picked up his pace, almost running. When he started to run, it became worse. It felt like someone was chasing him. He looked over his shoulder, the hair on the back of his neck prickles, and his heart raced. The next minute, he convinced himself there is nothing to be afraid of, so he slowed his pace in case anyone was watching. They'd see he was not afraid. He was courageous. He mounted the steps of the neighbor's house, knocked, and got the job done.

I miss the kid in the apple tree who loved to be in the kitchen with Mrs. Derstine. The kid climbed high up into the tree and shook it like he was the Hulk. She picked up the harvest of apples he's created. She began tucking the apples safely in the fold of her apron, when he giggles and shakes the tree again so apples fall on her.

The little devil.

I miss the kid that dared circumvent the cornfield and brave the demons in the woods. I miss the kid that helped carry his sibs to safety when the house caught fire, the kid that helped Mom when she had her tenth child. I missed the good son.

I missed the teenager who went to sock hops and hayrides. I missed the teenager who danced, with a girl named Luella, on the polished floor of the basketball court, and who tried to go so fast that they both fell into a pile of human laughter. The kid who blushed when a girl said hello and who thought he danced like Fred Astaire. I missed the actor who played Dobie and signed an autograph for Peter and Paul as if it was commonplace. I missed the kid who drove up on the sidewalk in Nana's car and the kid who could make mistakes and laugh and do better next time. I even missed the kid who wrestled to second place in the state tournament because his performance said it was not about failure or "I can't," but it was about who I am.

I wish I hadn't given up on that kid. I wish I hadn't listened to words that made me think he wasn't good enough. Instead, I chose the kid with the fat ass, the kid who was a coward and who couldn't make good decisions. I chose the poor athlete and the kid who wasn't going to amount to much. I saw these reflections in Dad's eyes, and they became me. It should never have been about what I thought Dad saw in me. It should have been about that brave, daring, devilish, helpful, and good kid. I gave up on that kid, and I abandoned him. I tried and tried to change the reflected picture of me, and it didn't work. I tried to be the son I thought Dad wanted. I should have realized that I had everything I needed, and I should have embraced me. I didn't. I just didn't know how much I would need that kid.

Chapter Five

WAR HUMOR

Our officer's club in Da Nang, a converted shed, may have been only twenty-by-twenty feet in size; if larger, I'd be surprised. We took over the shed, removed the tar paper and tools, installed a bar, just a makeshift shelf, and had the Seabees install the tile floor. This was the brainchild of our executive officer.

The Seabees, the Navy Construction Battalion, had a history of building bases, bulldozing and paving thousands of miles of roadway and airstrips dating back to World War II. So maybe asking them to design and construct our club was a bit presumptuous. The Seabees were paid with cases of San Miguel Beer. During our runs into Nam, when on R&R, or just on a beer run, we packed the EC-121 with San Miguel Beer to stock our "bar" and use as our monetary standard.

After the initial construction, which included tile the color of pea green soup on a white background, we decided to stain the walls of the club ourselves as a final touch. After all, it wasn't construction; we could handle this. The final product would be a true designer's claim to fame. We began thinking of calling *Architectural Digest* for a photo shoot.

A few of us began: we drank and stained, drank and stained, drank and drank and drank. I got sloppy and spilled stain on the new pea green soup tile, ruining about two squares of the new floor. My initial thoughts included, *I'm dead. The XOs going to kill me.* Mother Luck, however, graced me.

Illusions Are Wonderful

The Seabees had stored some excess tiles behind the shed and a can of the black glue used to cement the tiles down. With the help of my comrades, I pried up the two ruined tiles, scraped the cement slab under them, slavered on the glue, and fitted the two new squares into the open space. I then stomped down on the tiles, hard, very hard, so the glue would take.

Not being an expert on tile work, I had put too much glue under the new tiles, and as I stomped the black goo seeped up around the two-tile area and ruined an even larger area. Now I had ruined a four to six tile area. Not to be daunted, I pried up the newly ruined flooring, scraped the cement floor applied glue, less this time, and stomped with confidence.

My estimate of "less" still left a lot to be desired, and glue oozed again, ruining an area of eight to ten square tiles. I looked up and realized I was alone. My comrades had bailed. They wanted no part of this, and they didn't want to be around when the XO entered to survey our handiwork on his new cherished club. After one more failed attempt, I gave up. The clock read 3:00 a.m., and I had replaced half the floor. The half I replaced looked crooked, uneven, and haphazard like a drunk did it. The oozing black gunk had been scraped off the tiles, and the tiles washed and scrubbed as I tried returning them to their original pea green and white glory. The result was that it looked like an angry racehorse had shit on the pea green, pawed at the pile, and grazed over it for an eternity. I was tired, under the influence, and I had a mission the next morning.

I was hard-pressed the next day to disavow any knowledge of the ruined floor and not to laugh when my fellow tilers stated they were nowhere around the club that night. Someone must have broken in and damaged the premises. In exchange for more cases of beer, which I hated to part with, the Seabees came back, replaced the flooring, and returned the club to its intended poshness.

Sometime later, time was unimportant in this hellhole. I sat drinking alone in the officer's club. My crew and fellow officers had enough sense to stop drinking hours before and had wandered back to the barracks. The two-story structure with four weak wooden walls on a cement slab had been constructed on a barren field of brown dirt about one hundred yards from Shed Club. A low white fence had been erected at the end of the dirt field between the club and the barracks. It must have been added to break up the drab scenery and to create a storybook look to help us forget we were in a war zone.

I was drinking and feeling no pain when the rocket attack began. The first rocket landed close. The loud boom created a heightened sense of urgency. The safety of the bunker, an additional hundred yards away, the nearness of the first fuselage of rockets, and my state of mind did not prove comforting. I burst from the shed door and began to top the world record for the hundred-yard dash.

Da Nang had an additional menace, numerous stray dogs. Some looked friendly, some looked like they thought your arm would make a nice lunch, and some didn't even look. One big black mangy mutt hung out near us. To avoid the heat of the day, the dog would dig a narrow trough in the dirt between the barracks and the club and lie low in the cool earth below the surface of the field. Blind drunk, I raced across the dirt field in the dark, not aware of the big dark, black dog hunkered down for the night in his dark black hole. The dog, apparently desensitized to rocket attacks, snored totally unfazed by current events. As this hurdling mass of humankind approached the trough, the dog awoke, got territorial, reared up out of his pit, and howled. A heart-stopping howl that rivaled the mating call of a werewolf.

To avoid a physical confrontation with Mangy or just because he scared the shit out of me, I went airborne, screaming like a female member of the glee club. I flew several feet above Mangy and never saw the fence. I cleared it like a high hurdler with room to spare. I landed near the bunker where twenty or so men were fleeing to safety. I did not need a helmet for my privates as they had disappeared up into my stomach, threatening never to be seen again.

It appeared we had another freeze-frame moment. Everyone stopped their flight to the bunker and stared at me to see where I got hit and to assess my injuries. Maybe they were just looking to see the teenage girl newly deployed to Da Nang. As a leader, I recovered quickly. I mustered the deepest, huskiest voice I could. It sounded like I was talking from the bottom of a well. I ordered the men to keep moving and assured them no one was hurt. I did not realize the full range of my voice until that incident.

* * *

On one deployment, we visited Thailand for R&R. One of the flight crew hooked up with a lovely local beauty who wanted commissary privileges. Love was not the motivation for this infatuation. She was not swept off her feet by the crew member; she just wanted to buy cheap food, alcohol, and other goodies. I believe she thought because they had a one or two-night stand, for which he probably paid her handsomely, that she was entitled to a marriage license and military privileges.

We were about to depart the air base when the crew member raced onto the runway with his "intended" in tow, and the lovely lady wouldn't leave. She clung to our teammate like white on rice. I ordered the men to board the plane, but none complied. Everyone wanted to see how this drama unfolded. I spoke politely and firmly to the lady in question and asked her to leave. She too completely ignored me and refused to leave. She said that as partial payment for services rendered, the crew member had promised to marry her.

What We Won't Do for Love

As "captain" of the ship, I decided the only way to solve the predicament was to marry them. To clear up a few lingering issues, I am not the captain, and our aircraft is not a ship. I had no real authority to marry anyone, anytime, anywhere. Reality can be troublesome, but I didn't let that roadblock stop me. I grabbed a clipboard with a blank maintenance order on it, filled in their names, the date, time, and place of this sacred ceremony and proceeded to marry them. With all the solemnity I could muster, with the crew gathered around and his closest buddy as best man, I asked if they took each other to have and to hold until this day do us part or until we depart, whichever came first. Upon pronouncing them man and wife, I signed the work order and ripped off the pink copy for her. She snatched up the pink paper, dumped us like hot potatoes, and headed for the commissary at a trot. The last we saw of her was her dark hair and the pink marriage certificate waving in the breeze, high above her head. Shopping now number one.

The engines revved, the new husband, sans wife, but with his wedding party, or more aptly named, his crew boarded the aircraft and headed back to Vietnam. Not the garden spot for a honeymoon, but then there was no wife either. The crew applauded my Oscar-winning performance as the officiate of that masterful ceremony. Cry your eyes out, Dobie. Some of the guys might have thought it was real because they had tears in their eyes, or was that just from laughing?

* * *

One night, in Da Nang, I passed out cold on the floor. Not funny, and it wasn't from drinking. I remember abdominal pain just before the lights went out. I had to be airlifted to a field hospital via helicopter. It would have been nice if I had been seated or laid inside the air ambulance, but I was strapped to a pylon on the outside of that monster. The third beast infiltrating my life. I came to, looking up and seeing only the open sky blurred by a whirling rotor. I looked around and saw nothing but air. I might be nervous inside an aircraft, but I am more than terrified to be on the outside of one. I looked toward my toes, saw my boots strapped to my chest, and wondered what I did to deserve this. *Was I dead? Did I mess up another floor?* I didn't remember passing out. The helicopter flew over the jungle, and when it banked, I was sure I would be unceremoniously deposited on the jungle floor a few thousand feet below. I screamed like that glee club member again. I knew it was safe to do that because the roar of the engine was deafening, and no one around me was conscious. I felt the end had to be near when we approached the hospital for landing. The pilot turned hard to avoid trees, enemy fire, and anything else deemed threatening. We landed quick and hard.

During the twenty-four hours I was at the field hospital, we came under rocket attacks twice. All of us in the hospital were in bed with IVs and tied up with all kinds of wires. We couldn't race to a bunker pushing our IV stands. My symptoms eventually disappeared, all the symptoms except fear, and they released me to return to my squadron. The hospital staff had to treat those injured by bullets, rockets, and bamboo shafts, and I had none of those. A few days later, after being back on full duty, I had a repeat occurrence. This time, I was sent to the naval hospital on Guam. The doctors there determined I had appendicitis and that immediate surgery was required because it could burst at any moment.

I remember the prepping, being wheeled down the bright white hallway, waiting forever for something to happen, being in a room with four to six white-clad ghosts standing around my bed, mumbling and then lights out again. I have about the same level of fear for surgeries that I have for flying.

Not Having a Good Week

I began to surface from god knows where, slipping in and out of consciousness. I saw a white ceiling, fluorescent lights, and no open sky. I heard noises to my left. Slowly, I turned and vaguely saw a rotund brown man grinning at me. His mouth was moving, but I couldn't make out what he was saying. I sat bolt upright in bed, stitches and all, because there was a huge hole in the middle of his face. He had two eye sockets, a gaping mouth, and a huge hole where his nose should have been. I blinked and blinked, but the nose did not reappear. He was grinning and talking to me, and I thought, *I didn't make it. This had to be Satan's henchman.* I had been told I was going to hell, and it appeared I did.

Looking left did not appear to be in my best interest, so I turned right. In the bed on that side was a big white guy covered by a sheet. Something was off there too. His legs were bent with the soles of his feet flat on the mattress, his knees pointed toward the ceiling and spread wide like he was delivering a baby. *Now I'm sure there's no hope.* The guy said, "Yeah, dude, you think that guy on the other side is bad, look at this." He whipped back the sheet to reveal he was naked from the waist down. I didn't want to see him naked under any conditions. But worse yet, he was pointing between his legs at a monstrous black sack. Where most of us of the male species have this nice little sack with two, normally marble-sized balls rolling around in it, this man had a grapefruit-sized black package just lying on the sheet. He couldn't move, and I'm sure if he had tried to move that monstrous testicle would fall to the floor. That wasn't a scene I wanted to be a player in. I was in enough pain. I couldn't look left, and I couldn't look right. With no option left, I looked at the ceiling and hoped the nightmare would end soon.

More Drugs, Please

I couldn't ask the Guamanian what happened to his nose, and I couldn't ask the white dude what happened to his nuts, so I started babbling incoherently until someone came over to my bedside. Thinking I was in agony, the attendant upped my dose of painkillers.

Amen

I learned the lovely no-nose gentleman to my left was from a nearby island. His nose had been removed due to skin cancer. The plan was to retrofit him with a new nose when they were sure he was cancer-free. Where would they get the tissue to rebuild his nose? I didn't want to think about it.

The noise I heard had been him asking me if I needed anything. I was calling out rather loudly when I was going in and out of consciousness. The white gentleman to my right apparently had a vasectomy that went south on him, really.

Put That Thing Back Under the Sheet, Please

After we had three kids, Doris asked if I'd get a vasectomy. She never understood why I said no and raced screaming from the house. Years later, when I was told I had skin cancer, I looked in the mirror and saw a gaping hole in the middle of my face before they even got the knife out.

Welcome to mind over matter.

Chapter Six

LIES

"They've been shot down."

The "official" story about the shoot down didn't add up.

On April 15, 1969, North Korean shot down one of our EC-121 aircraft. *I tried not to think about it for forty-five years.* I locked up that conflict and the truth with all the atrocities and feelings of that era. I didn't have the strength to fight my own demons. I needed to keep my strength to stay alive. I couldn't squander it on the truth. Besides, I flew the same mission the day before they died...and some tried to blame me.

Flight logbook

MONTH	APRIL	YEAR	1969

CODES: A—Automatic, C—GCA, F—ADF, G—GCA, I—ILS, L—LF range, O—OMNI, R—Radar, Y—TACAN, S—Simulated, J—Jet

DAY	AIRCRAFT MODEL	SERIAL NUMBER	KIND OF FLIGHT CODE	PILOT TIME				SPECIAL CREW TIME	INSTRUMENT TIME ACT	SIM	NIGHT TIME	CARRIER				LANDINGS DAY/LAND	CATAPULT	SPD. INST. APPR. COMP. PLTTO			REMARKS
12	EC121M	143209	1V2					9.7													
13	EC121M	143209	1V5					9.0													
14	EC121M	143209	1V2					2.3													
15	EC121M	143209	1V2					2.9	.5												
16	EC121M	143209	2V2					8.6													
17	EC121M	143209	2V2					9.9	2.0												
18	EC121M	143209	1V2					5.3													
20	EC121M	143209	1V2					7.9	5.1												
21	EC121M	143209	1V2					2.3	1.2												
27	EC121M	143209	1V2					9.8													
28	EC121M	143209	1V2					9.5	1.1												
29	EC121M	143209	1V2					9.7	2.4												
30	EC121M	143209	1V2					8.1	1.2												

					13.5	CERTIFIED A CORRECT RECORD	
TOTAL THIS PAGE	105.0		105.0			Pilot	
BROUGHT FORWARD	90.0		70.8		3.9	Approved	
TOTAL TO DATE	195.0		175.8		16.9	C.O. or authorized deputy	

*See page 2 for codes — TOTAL ACCUM. PILOT TIME — TOTALS, THIS FISCAL YEAR — TOTALS, THIS FISCAL YEAR

Flight logs for April 1969

We took off from Atsugi, Japan, and flew along the southern coast of China and the eastern coast of North Korea, flying a routine SIGINT (signal intelligence) mission. The flight plan called for us to land in the Philippines after the mission, stay for a night, then continue to Vietnam for the duration of our deployment. We could not fly directly to Vietnam from Japan. America's treaty with Japan prohibited direct support of the war in Vietnam from air bases located in Japan.

Shortly after we turned south, my crew and I detected the active presence of MiG-21s in North Korea. These next-generation fighter aircraft were not just sitting idle on the runway. Intense training was being conducted, for the North Korean pilots, on the use of the air-to-air missile system. These aircraft were, in our best estimation, located at an air base near Wonsan. The blatant and overt transmissions of signals from the North

Koreans was unusual and meaningful. In our current Cold War with North Korea, they were very secretive. Reliable information was not easy to come by. They were training for something. They were up to no good.

This unusual discovery had a high intelligence value because prior to that date, we were not aware that North Korea possessed MiG-21s. We learned Russia had delivered these advanced fighter aircraft to North Korea and were training the pilots on how to operate the weapon systems. This significant upgrade to North Korea's arsenal was of concern locally and internationally.

While airborne over the Sea of Japan, I reported the discovery to headquarters in Atsugi. Our orders were immediately amended to deadhead to Vietnam. Do not stop. Do not pass go. Do not collect two hundred dollars. Do violate the treaty with Japan. Do put all the flight data, recordings, reports, and transcriptions together for immediate transfer to Atsugi. The crew we were replacing in Da Nang was ordered to wait for our arrival to transport the package back home.

The normal operational procedure for the crew on the ground in Da Nang was to take off as soon as they got a message from us. When we approached Da Nang, we would radio the departing crew that we were 100 percent. The aircraft, crew, and equipment were good to take over future missions in the Southeast Asia Theater. This allowed them to take off early to get on their way home.

Hours later, we landed. I ran to the waiting aircraft and passed on the sensitive and important documentation to the crew. Their engines were revved and ready because they overheard our approach on the radio. Almost before I cleared the hatch, they were rolling down the runway. It wasn't often we got advance notice of impending military operations, but something was up. This was the oracle of doom. Everyone knew it, and the urgency of those involved became evident.

A day or two later, as we're flying a mission over the Gulf of Tonkin, our pilot received a high-priority, classified message from HQ. The transmission ordered us to shut down all coded equipment and not use passwords or transmit anything of a sensitive nature. Not knowing why we had received this order baffled us. It rendered us useless for our current mission. I recommended we turn south and head back toward Da Nang and safety. We were flying blind.

Halfway back to base, the pilot told me, confidentially, that we had lost contact with a plane over the Sea of Japan. No one knew what happened to the aircraft and crew, and we did not know if any of our equipment or codes had been compromised.

After landing in Da Nang, we learned that, concurrent with our mission in Southeast Asia, another SIGINT crew with the call sign Deep Sea 129 flying over the Sea of Japan had been attacked and shot down by a North Korean MiG-21.

The United States denounced this "unprovoked" attack and claimed Deep Sea 129 was flying over international waters. The report went on to say the aircraft crashed 90 nautical miles (103 miles) off the coast of North Korea.

North Korea claims a twenty nautical mile sovereign airspace boundary off its coast. Most nations claim twelve nautical miles per the maritime definition of territorial waters.

According to North Korea, the US spy plane was attacked because it intruded into airspace claimed by North Korea. This blatant act of revenge and retaliation by North Korea for the airspace violation was heralded as a gift from the military leaders to the North Korean dictator on his birthday.

The verbal and unconfirmed reports, following the incident, were that a single air-to-air missile had been fired by the MiG-21, blowing Deep Sea 129 out of the sky. The North

Korean pilot then descended and strafed the remains of our aircraft with their .23 mm cannon. A Russian trawler, first on the
scene, helped retrieve the wreckage. In addition, the Russian
crew recovered two bodies. The only bodies of the crew ever
recovered.

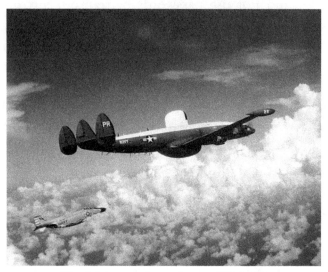

North Korean shoot down of EC-121

My unit was the US Navy's Fleet Airborne Reconnaissance
Squadron VQ-1, and we flew in support of the Seventh Fleet.
The missions to collect data and communications intelligence
were controlled by the Naval Security Group operated by the
National Security Agency. These missions were code named
Beggar Shadow. The US Air Force and Navy had flown more
two hundred similar missions between January and April
1969. We had been conducting missions off the coast of North
Korea for two years. This didn't make sense. Why did North
Korea choose to shoot down this plane, killing all thirty-one
Americans on board? Why did North Korea take this hostile

action that resulted in the single largest US aircrew loss during the Cold War? I warned them. I was going mad. Why?

North Korea immediately went on high alert, and within hours of the incident broadcast its version of the event. They referred to the tragedy as "the brilliant battle success of shooting it *(Deep Sea 129)* down with a single shot by showering the fire of revenge upon it." Deep Sea 129 was described by North Korea as "the plane of the insolent US imperialist aggressor army." The North Korean media accused the Americans of "reconnoitering after intruding deep into the (North Korean) territorial air."

This was the second incident in a little more than a year of aggressive behavior by North Korea against US forces. On January 23, 1968, the spy ship USS *Pueblo* was captured by the North Koreans. One crewman was killed, and eighty-two were captured, tortured, and held prisoner for eleven months. The North Koreans stated that US forces entered North Korean territorial waters several times to conduct espionage activities. Commander Lloyd Bucher taped a confession stating the USS *Pueblo* was in North Korean waters and not in international waters as the US claimed. This confession was broadcast via loudspeakers across the DMZ between North and South Korea to demoralize troops guarding that heavily fortified border. The North Koreans did the exact same thing with the Deep Sea 129 shoot down, broadcasting their "success" in downing the American spy plane. The effect was demoralizing and haunting to all US troops.

The North Koreans were blatantly aggressive, undisciplined, egotistical, and aloof; but they are not stupid. They knew the United States would not retaliate for either incident. From the reports and discussions, at that time, many of us believed Deep Sea 129, like the Pueblo, had intruded into North Korean claimed territory. Deep Sea 129 may have been ninety miles into international waters at the time it crashed into the water but why was it chased and shot down? Neither Lyndon Johnson nor Richard Nixon ordered any retaliation for these acts of aggression against US forces. Retaliation could not be justified if we were in the wrong and if we had intruded. The USS Pueblo is still held by North Korea, and is moored in Pyongyang as a museum. The plane and most of the crew of Deep Sea 129 remain somewhere in the depths of the Sea of Japan.

I challenged the powers to be over why Deep Sea 129 was up there in the first place. Why did they stray so close after I warned them about the MiG-21 activity? They said my tapes weren't very good and the brass needed additional evidence to support the presence and use of MiG-21s. They needed to be sure before briefing Washington. Deep depression overcame me; I had failed. Not enough intelligence; data not good enough, not recorded properly, not enough to prevent the loss of thirty-one lives.

Not the Soldier Dad Would Be Proud Of

A few months later, I found the tapes from my mission in the squadron's lab in a stack of tapes to be degaussed for reuse. I listened to them. They were clear and definitive. I got the squadron XO and, while hiding the mission number, played the tape for him, and asked what it sounded like to him. Thinking it was a training opportunity, he quickly said, "That's a MiG21." I told him these were my tapes; these should have been the warning needed to keep Deep Sea 129 at a safe distance. I also blurted out that neither he nor anyone else better ever say they weren't good enough again. I was in tears and completely deflated and demoralized. The tapes recorded a clear and loud wake-up call to danger. Unfortunately, the damage was done, and the loss of Deep Sea 129 weighed heavily on me for many years.

Additional reports stated that the crew of Deep Sea 129 had no clue they were under attack, that they were caught unaware, and the two bodies recovered were wearing only normal flight gear and had not donned parachutes or other survival gear. This preyed on my soul.

Those Statements Make No Sense

The crew of Deep Sea 129 had to know, based on the electronic capabilities aboard, that they were under attack. This was an unarmed, four-engine, prop-driven aircraft flying at nine thousand or ten thousand feet, and the MiG-21s had been airborne for more than an hour prior to the attack, according to the Army Security Agency located in South Korea. The commander of the flight had tried to take evasive action; he knew he was under attack. We ignored, or may have inadvertently breached, North Korea's declared territorial air space, and we created a situation in which we lost more troops. Some said the mission was scheduled with high-level people on board who wanted the distinction and rewards for discovering this activity and set themselves up as heroes. Instead, it killed them.

When incidents like this occur, a shroud of secrecy is cast over all of us connected to it. The Navy always wants to control the release of information and ensure the communication of the details is done by the appropriate sources. That also includes making sure the "right story" is released. My crew and I were sequestered in Da Nang, and we worried that our wives and families in Atsugi were about to hear that one of our planes was lost. Japanese radio picked up information like this in rapid fashion and would broadcast it immediately. Our families would not know what plane or what crew was shot down.

Panic would set in and flow like hot lava from Mt. Etna until they learned the truth. Then sighs of relief or sobs of pain would soar above Atsugi, depending on who was lost. We tried to take care of one another and the families of the men who were away. What can you do when you are ordered under threat of court martial not to discuss anything related to the incident with anyone?

My good friend and colleague Rich would check in with Doris and the kids from time to time when I was away. He was in Atsugi when the plane was shot down. He immediately went to the house on a "routine" visit. He was very bright, and he just invited himself inside despite any plans Doris may have had. He told her things like, "Yeah, I just talked with Joe, and he's doing fine. He's in Vietnam. He and the crew are doing good and should be home in about three weeks. They are really doing well..." and on and on until Doris wondered if he had dementia. She was suspicious. First, saying we were "fine" once was enough. Secondly, she asked Rich how he talked with me? Back then, we didn't have cell phones; we didn't even have landlines connecting us. Shortly after Rich left, Doris heard the news on the radio: a US plane stationed at Atsugi was shot down by the North Koreans in an act of retaliation. Initial panic was not completely avoided by Rich's visit, but it only lasted seconds, not hours or days. As Doris processed the news and fear started to invade her thoughts, she thought of Rich. Being bright herself, she figured out the reason for Rich's demented rant, and instantly realized, my crew and I were safe. She packed up the kids and, like all the concerned wives, headed to the base to help where she could.

Losses in 1968, 1969, and now in 1970. On March 16, a US spy plane crashed on landing in Da Nang, killing twenty-two crew members. Nine additional crewmen and two USAF men were injured. Most of the nine additional crew members were in the tail section of the aircraft that snapped off during the crash. The tail section ended up in a baseball field near a power plant. The two air force men were in or near the hanger the EC-121 crashed into. Rumor had it that a Vietnamese tar truck was motoring near the scene at the time of the crash. As the tail section bounced toward him, the driver stopped and exited the truck. Terrified by the sight of the tail section bouncing toward him, he started running, and we don't know if he was ever seen since. The tail came to rest in the field, the door opened, and some of the men crawled out.

Miracles in War

The reports stated the EC-121 "faltered…during its landing approach and crashed in flames into a hanger…" Military authorities attributed the crash to "mechanical failure." The plane didn't falter, the pilot did. The pilot in the left seat was not competent and should not have been flying the aircraft. It was true; the EC-121 had lost an engine while in route to Da Nang—one of four engines. The plane could still be flying today on three engines. It was not an emergency. That was a mechanical issue, but a competent pilot would not declare it an unmanageable, emergency situation. "Crashed in flames" should have read burst into flames after it crashed into a Quonset hanger.

Crash of EC-121 Da Nang
http://www.navyct.com/d_biglook.shtm

Engine issues and engine failures on EC-121s were not uncommon. As this pilot approached the runway in Da Nang, the tower notified him that the first one thousand feet of the runway was closed for construction and that he flew too low and too slow to clear the obstacles. They advised him to wave off and make another approach to ensure a safe landing. The pilot overreacted and went BTW (balls to the wall or full throttle). He applied full power to all four engines to gain altitude, circle the airfield, and make a second attempt to land. He forgot that one engine was out on the right side. With two engines at full throttle on the left side and only one on the right, the aircraft banked to the right, with the right wing down and the left wing pointed toward the sky. The aircraft began a sharp right turn low to the ground, and before they could recover the tail section hit the ground, the right wing caught the roof of a Quonset hut housing an F-4 Phantom fighter-bomber. The

F-4, ready for action with multiple bombs attached, and the front half of the EC-121 were destroyed. The tail section, still pretty much intact, snapped loose and flew into a field. Twenty-two dead and eleven injured.

The pilot was going to have his wings pulled. He was failing as a pilot. He didn't have the aptitude or skill to fly. That shouldn't be shameful, but it was. This pilot was not the commander of the mission to Da Nang. The commander convinced the authorities in Atsugi to give this pilot one more chance. He argued he would take the failing pilot on this mission, instruct him, coach him, and give him one last chance to prove himself. If the failing pilot was successful, he could keep his wings and be given command of his own aircraft on future missions. The commander was successful in getting the authorities to allow the failing pilot a second chance, but he lost his life, being the "good guy".

Rich's crew had relieved my crew in Nam, and I was back in Atsugi. Rich's wife, Carol, was in Japan alone. I rushed to her house to find her in a state of panic. She'd already heard the news of the crash, and she didn't know if it was Rich's plane that went down. We had the same communications restrictions levied on us as before, and I was only allowed to leave base moments before I arrived at Carol's home. Following Rich's example, I told Carol that I was not authorized to talk about any incident. I could neither confirm nor deny the loss of another aircraft and crew, but I told her enough that shortly after I left, it hit her that Rich was safe.

Welcome to Grief That Spans Generations

It wasn't over with the Da Nang crash. I was back on the base when the wives of the men lost were told of the tragedy and the death of their husbands. In times like these, when a family is stationed overseas, the Navy assigns a Casualty Assistance

Claims Officer, or CACO, to each family. The job of a CACO is to assist the relatives of the men lost with any benefits due, with packing and moving back to the States and just being there to assist until they got home to loved ones. I was assigned to help the family of the third pilot on board the crashed EC-121. The third pilot was a good friend and confidant, who was always there for me when we flew together. One particularly bad night in Nam, he just held me. He was of strong, silent German stock and was steadfast in the performance of his duties. Silently and firmly, he shared his strength, and through that gesture, I came to believe we would make it through another night. Unfortunately, he didn't make it through this night.

He left behind two young boys. I rushed over to his house to support his wife, Sherry, and the boys. As I approached her house, I heard screaming and wailing and cursing. I heard enough to know Sherry blamed the other pilot for her loss, and she held back no thoughts or adjectives in describing him and his attributes. I was walking up the sidewalk when she burst through the screen door and raced down the path toward the home of that pilot. That pilot's wife, in the same morass of grief, would not appreciate nor did she deserve this confrontation. Words did not deter Sherry, and I had to physically grab her and hold her tight. She fought like a trapped demon, and down we went onto the lawn, rolling about like fighting teenagers. I just held on and tried to console her. I was black and blue before she settled down out of sheer exhaustion. Dejected, with our heads slumped, we slowly walked back to her house. Our limbs were aching, and we were spent from the physical and mental toll of the ordeal.

I helped her with the paperwork and helped her pack. The days passed sadly but uneventfully. Often, I would take the boys out to play or go for a walk and give Sherry time to mourn, to pack, and sort through her memories. One evening near dinnertime, I was sitting in the living room with the boys. They now knew their father was dead. They were so young. I didn't know Sherry told them, and I'm not sure that was a good idea, but it wasn't my decision. They were handsome blond, blue-eyed boys of three or four, and they too were sad. Sad only in the way a child can be sad when they don't comprehend the magnitude of the situation. They just knew Mommy was very, very sad. The older boy stopped playing, came to my knees, looked up into my eyes, and told me his daddy was dead. I told him I knew and picked him up and put him on my lap. He stared at me with those big blue eyes and gently asked, "Are you going to be my daddy now?" I don't know if you can hear a heartbreak, but I certainly heard something that day that still echoes in my memory.

I didn't know Sherry had come out of the kitchen and was leaning against the doorframe watching, listening, and wondering where to go from there. I gently told the boy I couldn't be his dad, but I'd be his friend, and I'd be there for him if he needed anything. With the innocence of a child, he thanked me and rested his head against my chest and silently sobbed. I wasn't quite so silent. I put them on a plane a few days later, waved goodbye, and have never seen them since. I went home and held my girls until I thought they would break.

The pain caused by trauma, loss, and war has a broad reach. The pain of those who were injured is obvious. But pain spans generations. Those boys will live a different life. It's hard for me to comprehend. Would they be okay? How would their new life unfold? Even if they didn't know it, at that moment, life as they knew it ceased, and a new struggle began. The heart hurts, and those hurt do anything to stop the pain. What would they do? I know what I did, and the pain didn't go away; it was just masked, waiting until a quiet moment or the dark of night when it would slip back, and I'd hear the echo of his voice asking, *Are you going to be my daddy now?*

Chapter Seven

NOWHERE TO TURN

*The Worst Element of War Might Be
What Happens After It's Over*

It was 1971. I was twenty-six years old, and it was over. I couldn't go back and pick up the shattered pieces of my life. The road forward was hell and would surely lead to my death. War didn't kill me, but the conflict within may. I knew what hell was. It's the chasm between the reality of me and the perception of what Dad wanted me to be, groomed me to be, and prematurely celebrated in his dreams. I was the coward, the failure, and the guy who came in second.

A letter to Dad that was never sent:

Dear Dad,

Christmas 1971

I want so badly to be the person that makes you proud. I work hard, act with courage, succeed and think I'm closing that gap and gaining ground but I see reflected in your eyes nothing's changed. I feel like there is a dark river between us. A dark river that may swallow me. You are on the opposite shore and I'm trying to reach you. I think I see you looking at me but it's not me your seeing. It's the person you wanted me to be.

My lifeline had been the thought that I could always come home. When the fear got too real and the loneliness too dark, I could always go back home. The awareness that this was no longer an option created terror. I can't tell you about the conflict so severe it's tearing the tissue from my soul. A visceral pain I feel every day, with no balm to soothe or antidote to reverse the truth. It's no longer as simple as a fear of flying. It's a fear of living.

My world is like a pool with a vanishing edge. I can't see where the water came from or where it is going. The horizon is a distant mirage that keeps changing before my eyes. It changes because it's not real.

I felt like the script of my life had been written for me and it couldn't be edited. The experiences of my life have changed that pre-ordained script, and I can't fulfill the legacy of your hopes for me. Many said pick up the pieces, pull yourself up by your bootstraps, get over it, and just go on. Go on like nothing happened; like nothing changed. I've changed and not in ways you wanted.

I hate to admit it but I am drinking, drinking a lot. The conflict between who I was, who I've become, and the me of my family's hopes and dreams is like a vice. That vice tightens day by day. I drink every day and every night to get momentary relief from the pressure, to block the truth, and to lament the fact, there seems to be no way forward or no way home.

I can't see a future and I don't know a standard to measure me by. There is no way for you to say I love you. Mom sits silently signing Birthday cards and Christmas cards saying,

Love,
Mom and Dad

But never holding me and saying it out loud. She might as well have given the cards to the milkman. You only see the person that left three years ago. You see the image in the photo and think I survived. Did I?

I am not the son you wanted.

And never will be.

Love,
JF

It shouldn't end this way, can't end this way.

PART TWO

The Day Before I Died

I'm not afraid my life will end.
I'm afraid it will never start again.

Chapter Eight

THE HOMECOMING

1971

Time to leave Vietnam. Time to come home to the tumultuous decade of the seventies. I contemplated leaving the Navy. With a wife, three children, no job, no sense of confidence, and no me, it seemed formidable. Where could I go? What could I do? All I felt was loss and grief. All I heard was the echo of loneliness, and I couldn't envision tomorrow.

The fear about going home was that the war had ripped away my innocence and all my personal defenses. It was hard to fathom and even harder to explain. Understandably, most people didn't get it. Only those who experienced it knew what it was like and could possibly relate although each veteran had their own unique experience and reactions. When I tried to tell someone, anyone, I saw the patronizing "oh yes" in their eyes, and I heard platitudes that didn't help. I walked away, feeling like the damaged returning vet.

The loss of innocence is probably the worst. As a result of being in a combat zone and exposed to a high level of conflict, I experienced things I never thought possible. If I had had known what awaited me, I would have said, "No, thank you. Please let me remain ignorant of these realities." I'm not talking about the innocence of youth and childhood. When I hear the word innocence, I often think of my first sexual experience. That may seem simple in this context, but it was a normal rite of passage. I did not walk away from that experience and proclaim, "I am no longer innocent." I may have thought I was a man now, except for that clumsy part where I didn't know what I was doing. Experiences like those are the things I'd hoped for and, in some cases, prayed for because I knew it was part of a common baseline or normal life experience. After my first sexual experience, I could share with my confidants or partner and laugh at my mistakes with congratulatory hugs. But when the experience is not part of a common baseline or common social experience, it's a new ball game.

The traumas of war are experiences few shares and fewer understand. Some think it's the memory of what happened, but it's more than that. I can't erase it or replace it by conjuring up a vision of a pastoral setting. It's more than a sound that can be blocked by therapy. It's a new reality that I can't share, and I can't shed. My everyday world now didn't share my new baseline, and it never went dormant because it was the new order of me. That new unshared order became heavy. My world began to shrink, smaller and smaller. The lights began to dim, and the darkness grew as if creating a false cocoon of comfort and perceived safety.

Innocence Shattered with No Defenses Left to Combat the Demons of Uncertainty

My personal defenses were stripped from me on the battlefield, so when I tried to combat the demons within, I failed. My first attempt was to try to compartmentalize and put the bad thoughts and feelings way, way in the back of my mind into a sealed vault. This also failed because I couldn't separate the good from the bad. The struggle was so overwhelming. The pressure was building. The best I could do was to lock everything up.

When I saw a beautiful child, I didn't see a lollipop in her hand; it was a hand grenade. When I dwelled on a sunset over a beautiful field of flowers in the periphery of my vision, I saw the land mines next to the flowers. I lost the beauty of the Far East, the first years of a marriage, and the birth of children before I lost a sense of self and purpose. I couldn't reach excitement, I couldn't feel joy, and I had no gratitude for the life I was given and the fact that I survived.

Frequently, I attempted to justify, rationalize, or make it not my fault. It didn't matter. Love, courage, and strength were ebbing at an alarming rate. My vital resources receded because of the emotional journey the war demanded. With no roadmap to my future, I was lost. No one could relate or say, "I understand." No one could empathize, and no one could say it was going to be okay, so the pain grew exponentially. The journey from sheer terror to rowdy camaraderie, from feeling parental and protective to helpless and lost, from loving to losing love took its toll. I locked up my love for Doris, for me, for everyone and everything. I was bleeding courage and strength. I weakened and couldn't keep the darkness away. I was afraid to try to create a new world because that seemed so radical. So I pretended all was well. I created a life of make-believe, and I retreated into the safety of a small existence shrouded by darkness.

The simple answer eluded me. I had to start over. Build a new me and a new life. Maybe I could build a new life, but building a new me wasn't quite so easy. It wasn't like starting with a blank canvas. I had to unlearn the past. Forget and strip all that I was and hopefully relearn, rebuild, and find a new reality. I feared when the old me was gone and the new me not yet built, I'd just be nothing. Would the reality match the feelings? Would I just cease to exist?

Maybe with love, courage, and strength, I could have created and lived in a new reality. I could have adjusted and survived if only those resources weren't depleted or locked out. I didn't need to pretend the war didn't happen. I was dying to be taught how to be strong again; I was struggling to find love and acceptance. I needed a community that understood and unconditionally loved and respected me. I needed to own my current reality. I didn't need to forget; I just needed that love and that courage and that strength to make peace with my past. What baffled me was how could I survive in combat and fall so short on the streets of home.

Disconnected and Blind to Hope

I left for Vietnam feeling unloved, with the tide of the times and emotions in the United States, I was destined to come home and feel even less loved. I used all my courage to stand firm and not run in the face of fire. Through the remaining days of the seventies, I would wake in the middle of the night, worrying and trying to remember if I locked the doors. I wasted countless minutes trying to convince myself I was safe. It was a nightly ritual to lock up the house before bed, but I didn't trust myself. The uncertainty drove me to get up and roam the house, going from door to door and window to window, making sure my environment was locked, and hopefully, I was safe. My world had become so small I couldn't afford to have anyone steal even a glimmer of it. For most people, it probably doesn't take every ounce of strength to rise in the morning, open a door, and head out into your day. But when you've been fighting for years, it's a monumental task.

The next level of hell was when the feelings I had locked in the vault began to leech out. I tried to numb those bad memories and the troublesome feelings, not the good ones, with alcohol, my drug of choice. I tried to find solace and strength to quiet the troubling emotions and rebuild a cache of positive emotions, but I couldn't. I did not want to be, and tried not to be, a victim. Being a victim of circumstances, a victim of personal traits or loves and likes, was worse than war. It was an internal hell, and so I kept searching and medicating. My drug of choice worked but only for a short period. I ended up becoming a victim of alcohol.

I thought if I blunted the negative, the positive would surface and I'd be happy again. Unfortunately, alcohol numbed every feeling. I didn't know you can't use alcohol or drugs and selectively choose which emotions, which memories, and which events you're going to block. At first, I accepted the absence of the harsh and awful memories, but eventually I realized there was no joy, no happiness, and no new memories of life happening around me. Strength, love, and courage come from what we create today. They are not rewards for what we did yesterday. Love today and be loved. Stand strong in the face of today's problems and strength builds. Have courage that you can make it no matter what.

The world does not have to be bigger than today.

Alcohol was not my friend. It turned on me and robbed me of the desire to go on. It robbed me of the love, courage, and strength I was seeking and deceived me into believing it was making me strong, giving me the courage to go on and be happy. The smile was false, the courage only lasted until the next drink, and any strength was rapidly faltering.

It's not that I didn't want to live; I just didn't have the strength to live. I can't even say that I wasn't loved; Doris did her best; my family tried. It was just that I couldn't feel loved. In my darkness, my reality grew from I'm not the son you wanted to I'm not the brother, the friend, the husband, the father, or the soldier you wanted, so how could I be loved? I felt that way even before the war, those feelings now emerged stronger and more powerful. My foundation was shaky from the onset. Could I start over? In this new reality, all hope was lost. Hopelessness is not the foundation of a new reality.

I wanted acceptance, but I couldn't tell anyone about my world or ask for support. Acceptance, a powerful gift, eluded me.

* * *

Long after the marriage failed, my daughters, now in their teens, lived with their mom and stepdad. They often called me to say they were running away from home. Sometimes together and sometimes separately, they would threaten to bolt. I asked them why, and the response always had something to do with their perception of the unrealistic restrictions of the household's religion. "We can't do this or that, we're not allowed to wear that, and we can't watch MTV." So the girls would say, "We're out of here. Do you approve?" I always responded with a firm and resounding "no." They got really upset and engaged in a verbal tirade to change my answer. I would repeat, "I do not approve of you running away. I think you should sit down with your mom and stepdad. Discuss the problem and find a solution."

The consensus they reached seemed to be that I didn't know what I was talking about and they were going out the window anyway. Then I would say, "Call me when you get wherever you're going. I want to know you are safe." That astounded them. What they didn't understand was the difference between approval and acceptance. I didn't approve of them running away, but I accepted their decision, and I was here to help. Help them through the window and down the road, wherever it leads.

In my perception, I wasn't approved of or accepted. Nothing I was and wanted to be was enough, and that made it difficult to rise, open the door, and head out to face reality. Having experienced trauma, I went on high alert. It wasn't just the war or the sights or the sounds, I survived that, but at what cost? No one really knew how to assess the price of war. We can't assess what has truly been lost. I was more afraid of something else going wrong than of the dreams and memories. If I was faced with another challenge or another trauma, could I survive? I felt weak and spent. I didn't know if I could handle what was to come next. That haunted me and followed me like a stalker.

Since I wasn't good enough, to begin with, and experienced a significant depletion of resources, I was certain I could not handle what life threw my way. I had no power. That fear created more trauma than war itself. What was next? Would I survive? Did I fight and survive only to face the next challenge and have no armor to protect myself? Anytime I headed out the door, I needed to see everything, to hear everything, and to be on constant alert for the next attack. My senses surged, my skin tingled, and all my reactions were physical as well as mental. The effort and expenditure of strength it took just to go to the grocery store would be unimaginable to others. Being hyper-vigilant was exhausting, and so I shut down. I got tired, I got lonely, and I tried what I could to shut out the world and build up a reservoir of love and strength—to find the courage to rise, to open the door and head out again even if it was only to buy oranges. Shutting down and isolating resulted in a disconnection from everyone and everything.

I Realized I Couldn't Do It Alone

I had nowhere to turn. Based on that realization, I worried if I didn't find an answer, I would just head out of life itself. I contemplated suicide often. This dark existence was so close to death it didn't seem like a big step. It didn't seem very different. It wouldn't take much strength. I felt like I was nothing, I had nothing, and nothing was not much to give up. Nothing is the absence of everything, so why not?

No matter how strong or defiant I tried to be, this perception created additional barriers I had to overcome daily. I felt it was wrong to contemplate suicide—worse to do it. Did I want the easy way out? The dim light of today and the small world I had created were competing against the past that was no more. There was no strength in the memory of me. There was no courage in the accomplishments of the past, and I couldn't feel the love that was extended to me. I didn't consider suicide because I wanted to die; it was because I wanted the pain to stop, and I didn't think I could start a new life. I didn't think the loneliness of nothing could be filled with love and hope ever again. This struggle sapped more of my strength. I wanted strength to hug those I loved, to give them a shoulder to cry on, to create new adventures and new memories that promoted joy and happiness. All strength should not have had to be dedicated just to survive. *I needed to create a new me. A me I could be proud of and, most importantly, respect.*

The Struggle to Survive

Not being accepted is the basis of bullying. I was insulted and deeply hurt. I wasn't asking anyone to understand, and no one had to relate. Just accept me as I am. The new reality I now carried in every fiber of my being was alien to most. The reality of me wasn't accepted before, and now it certainly felt impossible. I could barely accept it without my drug of choice, alcohol. I had an even bigger secret. With that "other" secret, I knew acceptance was not in the cards. So I went within, I went silent, and I went home, not sure of anything anymore, and most importantly, not aware of who or what I was becoming. The fear of the unknown me overshadowed the fear of not being enough.

Welcome to My Personal Prison!

When we came home in the early seventies, we came home physically, but not mentally and emotionally. The truth is, we were never really brought home at all.

We had a plane ride, a new assignment, and a new awareness that made it almost impossible to reintegrate back into the family or the society we left. It was impossible because we had changed, and those who awaited our homecoming didn't.

Radical changes had happened in our persona and in our perception and views of the world around us. Combat veterans and belief systems were shattered and life, as they knew it, was altered. Dad still had the newspaper in front of his face and talked through it, Mom continued to watch *The Young and the Restless*, *The Price is Right*, or *This Is Your Life* in black and white. Nothing wrong with that, we all did it. I just resented those that were close to me for being the same as when I left. Why didn't they change so they could relate? If they understood they could hold me and say we'll make it through the night?

When we arrived stateside, we couldn't wear our uniforms in public because people jeered and called us "baby killers." We were spit on and unilaterally blamed for all the atrocities that occurred in Vietnam. That negativity was increased exponentially after the massacre at My Lai in 1968. American troops went into this small village and brutally shot everyone in sight. Hundreds of men, women, and children were killed. In the baseline we shared prior to Nam, everyone would say that was horrible, and I would agree. It never should never have happened, and I agree. The obvious and inevitable follow-up statement came nearly 100 percent of the time, "I don't understand how that could have happened," and this is where our beliefs diverged. We no longer agreed because I understood something as hideous as that, because that was now *my* new baseline. I didn't want to and couldn't share my new truth. If I did, then I would become that monster, and I didn't want to be anyone's monster.

Travelers to other countries regularly experience young children selling them gum and candy and having cute conversations and possibly snapping a selfie with the kids. In Vietnam, children, or those who looked like children, were trained to throw grenades into buses, shops, and restaurants. We put screens on our bus windows so the grenades bounced back and didn't sail through the open windows and come to rest on the floor at our feet. We'd sit with our backs to a wall in restaurants and have an exit strategy mapped out in case someone threw a grenade through the door. In that environment, we lost the stereotype of childish innocence; we lost the distinction between men, women, and children. In the extreme, we didn't see humans anymore; we just saw the *enemy*. These soldiers went into My Lai and killed the enemy, not men, women, and children. It is a subtle but powerful distinction. We are taught to defend and fight the enemy. In some instances, our orders dictated that we kill the enemy, but we should never and would never kill innocent men, women, and children. I don't expect anyone to understand that, and because I don't expect that, I can't share it, and I continued with my silence.

* * *

I think about the mass murders that happen with growing frequency these days, and I wonder if there is a similarity. Did the people responsible kill men, women, and children, or did they kill the enemy?

In 2012, Adam Lanza killed his mother, twenty children, and six educators, then himself at Sandy Hook Elementary School in Newton, Connecticut. Were they teachers and children to him? It was reported that Lanza had a "scorn for humanity" and was socially isolated and obsessed with mass murders. In his mental state, who did he kill? We look at the how, the why, and the who from our own perspective, not the perspective of the shooter. We haven't changed.

In 2018, nineteen-year-old Nikolas Cruz killed seventeen young students and staff members of Marjory Stoneman Douglas High School in Parkland, Florida. Nikolas wanted to be "a professional shooter," and in his mind, he became one. In high school, his fellow students avoided him. He had lost both of his adoptive parents. He may also have had mental issues and been autistic. His lawyer described him as "a broken child." Did he strike back at the enemies of his abandonment?

In the same year Cruz launched his attack, fifty-six-year-old Cesar Sayoc sent sixteen pipe bombs to his enemies. He identified his enemies as Democratic opponents of Donald Trump. He warned us of his enemy targets in photos plastered on his van. There did not seem to be a question. In Sayoc's eyes, these Democrats were no longer people but simply enemies that must be eliminated.

Robert Bowers wanted "all Jews to die." On October 27, 2018, he walked into the Tree of Life Synagogue in Pittsburgh, Pennsylvania, and shot eleven worshippers to death. To the forty-six-year-old Bowers, Jewish people were his enemy. In his worldview, "they were committing genocide to his people." Bowers also believed Jews were helping migrants from refugee caravans enter the country illegally. He called the refugees "invaders" and considered them violent. He stated, "I…can't sit by and watch my people get slaughtered."

From their perspective, I don't think murderers like these believed they were attacking innocent people. They thought they were taking out the enemy. To us, the victims were and are all innocent. I don't claim to have the answer, but maybe if we could identify the moment humans became objects or enemies to these killers, we could avoid more tragedies. Cesar Sayoc told us with the pictures on his van. Robert Bowers and Nikolas Cruz posted warnings online, and we didn't hear. We didn't see how those signs translated to actions and death. We haven't changed, and they did.

Have we traded the destructive elements of Vietnam, Agent Orange, the rockets and the bullets for toxic rhetoric and hollow-point words? Have we defined the "enemy" for those individuals living in a fantasy, mental illness, PTSD, or obsession? The warning signs were there, and we didn't recognize them, or we failed to deal with them. Maybe we just pushed them over the edge.

We were silent.

* * *

My new reality didn't even agree with me, but it's permanent. It doesn't make it right. I don't know how I would have reacted at My Lai; I wasn't there. But forty-five years later, I still sit in a restaurant with my back to the wall, facing the door so I can see if anyone throws a grenade through the door. And I have my exit strategy planned.

Forty-five years later, I am still silent because you don't need as much courage and strength to keep the doors of your secrets closed. It required less strength to stay locked up in my mind than it did to convince others to understand and accept. I know when I was lost; I had no way forward. When I looked back, all I saw was sorrow. It's not good to look back and see only sorrow or to look around and be clothed in the worry of today. The devastating part of being lost is not to see a future. The forest of my tomorrows was so dense, no light penetrated to lead me forward.

The greatest challenge of the homecoming was the total disconnection from everyone and everything. In Vietnam, no one knew what to expect or what to do next. We were a family of men. Men who understood. Men who shared their courage and strength. Men who did whatever was necessary to ensure we'd all make it through the night. It wasn't the gender that was important. It was the shared experience. It was the connection and the ability to learn, even when we didn't know what we were doing. We had each other to lean on and shared a common, although unusual, experience. We spoke the same language, learned the nuances of a look or a slight movement, and took the hits for one another. We did things we didn't know how to do with courage and confidence instilled by standing side by side with peers. We learned as we ran and flew and ducked and yelled.

The saving grace was to share that common experience with an immediate and transparent depth. These men shared the same reality, and they didn't question my reality with words or looks. This created more of a collective hero and less of a singular hero. But this was not the family I returned to. I had expectations that when I came home, I would fit in somewhere. I was sure I would be recognized, understood, and accepted. I came home alone. I couldn't bring those men with me, and the connection, my lifeline, was broken.

* * *

Knowing what I now know, I would still volunteer to go back. Not because I'm a hero. I no longer want to be the hero. I just don't want my grandchild to see the things I saw, hear the things I heard, and see their reality so harshly altered that it invokes silence. I don't want to look into their eyes and see the reflections of a new awareness or the new reality that I have. I want to see their innocence, the protective shell of normalcy, and the ability to go forward in life or back in memories as they see fit. Maybe that's the freedom we fight for. The freedom to remain innocent, the freedom to hope and to love, and the freedom to dream of a tomorrow that is bright and full.

I don't know how I got to this darkness. I don't know how my world got so small. I came from *Ozzie & Harriet* and *Leave it to Beaver* with the Cleaver family. I came from a protected, demanding, rigid, and religious life but a full bright and happy place. I was planning on building a bright and happy future. There was everything to look forward to, and then the darkness descended.

* * *

The Navy offered me an assignment at the Air Force Special Communications Center at Lackland Air Force Base in San Antonio, Texas. The assignment was to analyze, in real time, the loss of B-52 bombers in North Vietnam. The effort was a joint Navy and Air Force operation. I would be one of nine naval officers assigned to this task force. B-52s were being shot out of the sky like quail on the opening day of hunting season. The Navy had recently spent $52 million on each of the new Northrop Grumman Prowler EA-6 aircraft equipped with a pod mounted AN/AQL-99 jamming system designed to protect US aircraft on these bombing missions over Hanoi. It wasn't working as planned and designed. The number of US prisoners of war grew geometrically. I agreed to the assignment for two years and was glad to pad the transition back home with those two years. Things weren't good on the job front at home, and I felt this was an important assignment. We lost fifty-five thousand men in Vietnam and more than two hundred thousand injured. Enough was enough.

Welcomed to the Transition.

Traveling with three small children anywhere can be challenging. We had to fly from Agana (now called Hagåtña), Guam, to San Antonio, Texas. Our first layover was in Hawaii to refuel and then on to Los Angeles on the same plane. Unfortunately, I had to be in San Antonio ASAP, so we continued from Los Angeles to San Antonio with no rest. We packed up and boarded our plane for the first early morning leg of our journey. We got comfortably settled on the aircraft with the three little ones. Saying we were "comfortably settled" is a stretch since we were three kids and two adults in only four seats, and comfort was not the Navy's priority. Times were tough. As the engines roared to life, the noise woke two of the slumbering children who broke into a ceaseless fit of screaming to vent their displeasure. This went on for a very, very, *very* long time. Our fellow passengers stared at us with that "look." I'm sure everyone knows that look that says, "Could you please take those kids outside and play. At thirty thousand feet."

Doris finally settled the kids down, got them back to sleep mere minutes before we arrived in the garden paradise of Hawaii. Knowing this was the same aircraft we would fly to Los Angeles, we breathed a sigh of relief and planned our strategy with the kids as the plane refueled. I would take the only child awake with me and stretch my legs in the terminal while Doris remained on board with the sleeping angels. The aircraft settled on the tarmac smoothly and was rolling toward our gate when the pilot announced everyone must deplane while they refuel. I turned to look at Doris, and I recognized that "look." It's was pasta on the boobs again. The military is going to have to develop new procedures around refueling.

I grabbed my charge and headed down the aisle as I heard Doris tell the stewardess she wouldn't be waking the children and deplaning. Now I'm not sure who was crankier. Both people had just endured a long flight, and the crew wanted a moment or two in the terminal to grab a coffee or a snack and get a good stretch as well. I only heard the beginning of "Yes, you are," "No, I'm not," and "Yes, you are" because I'd gone to higher ground. Is someone going to ask her to cut the cake and find the ring again?

I strolled comfortably around the airport for most of the two-hour layover? I just survived a war zone, and I was not going to face a conflict with the flight crew or my wife. I enjoyed the open spaces, the shops, people watching, and playing with my oldest daughter, Debby. Time neared to reboard our aircraft, and we headed toward the appropriate gate. Hundreds of yards short of the gate, I heard a familiar cacophony of screaming that sounded like my offspring. Doris sat in an uncomfortable rust-colored plastic chair in the gate area. She had a blanket wrapped around all three of them and was glaring at me like I should have known she would lose the battle with the steward- ess. Funny, I had my money on her.

We landed in Los Angeles late and began the rush to a different terminal to make our connection to San Antonio. We had a Navy peer waiting in San Antonio to pick us up, take us to our new lodging, and support us in our transition to the new assignment. We couldn't miss this flight. We headed down ramps and through terminals on foot at breakneck speed. We had divided the carry-on baggage equally between us. I had two kids, three diaper bags, two adult carry-on bags, and the blanket we stole. Doris had one child by the hand and her purse. They strolled like they were in Central Park on Sunday.

We arrived in San Antonio, and I headed off to work the next day happy for the easier routine. Analysis began, and day after day, we received all the flight data information, all the intelligence intercepts by my former team, and anything we could lay our hands on to try to determine why our bombers were incurring such heavy losses.

The B-52s would fly a pattern north over Laos or the Gulf of Tonkin, remaining over landmasses considered safe or over water until the last possible moment, and then make a sharp ninety-degree turn either from the east or the west and head for Hanoi. The navy jammer aircraft were supposed to protect the B-52s by jamming the guidance signal of the surface-to-air missile system (SAM) operated by North Vietnam. Unfortunately, many of our bombers were shot down before they made the target.

The Soviet Union had supplied North Vietnam with the SA-2 missile system and provided more than fifteen thousand personnel as "advisers." The Soviet Union was trying to maintain its tentative relations with the United States, so overt support of North Vietnam wasn't wise. The advisers were supposed to be only training North Vietnamese troops on the use of the SAM missiles, but many of them were operating the systems. When they were operating the weapon systems, the Russians wore North Vietnamese Army uniforms to keep their actions clandestine.

Prior to the introduction of the SA-2 system, the North Vietnamese air defense system could only defend against low-altitude targets. This new system had a range of twenty-one miles and traveled at four times the speed of sound. Its 288-pound fragmentation warhead created much havoc with our aircraft and losses mounted. More than a dozen B-52s and their crew members were lost to these nearly five-thousand-pound missiles launched from truck-mounted systems. The system was extremely effective and, in the past, had been responsible for shooting down Gary Powers as he flew his high-altitude U-2 spy plane over Russia in 1960.

The missions over Hanoi were authorized as a result of the failed peace talks in Paris. The international community rallied against this campaign, and it came to be known as the Christmas Bombings. Why was the Navy jammer not effective enough to prevent the loss of these forces? Why was that a Christmas not to remember?

After weeks of analysis of pouring over the data and looking for a pattern, we hit pay dirt. In routine operations, the SAM system would pick up an approaching aircraft, track it for a segment of the flight, then lock on and fire. We observed that the missile launchers were not tracking or moving during the B52 runs. They remained stationary aimed at the exact coordinates where the B-52s turned to enter North Vietnamese territory. The B-52s made their predictable ninety-degree turn, the missiles locked on with ease, avoiding the difficult task of tracking and anticipating the route. They were successful, and our losses were statistically higher than anticipated.

We realized the design of Navy EA-6B jamming signal had a "hole" in its coverage. When the bombers made the ninety-degree turn, they were visible, vulnerable, and an easy target for the missile team. With this insight, the flight path was altered to avoid the sharp angle turns, and mission results improved significantly. In addition, Northrop Grumman reviewed and changed its jamming pattern to avoid any holes in coverage.

* * *

When not analyzing data, I was at home in our two-story white house with black trim. It was a very nice house in a tranquil neighborhood. The backyard had a large bed of roses in a garden shaped like a T, with the cap of the T running along the back fence. I spent hours tending to the flowers, pruning, fertilizing, and watering them. There were many different varieties, colors, and scents. It was relaxing and took away thoughts of war for just those few moments. Many families lived in the neighborhood, and it felt safe for us and our children.

One day, our oldest daughter, Debby, who was about four at the time, did not like her chores or was reprimanded for something. I don't really remember what lit the fuse, but she got in a huff and headed to her room. Moments later, she stomped down the stairs, clutching two pairs of underwear and a bathing suit. She boldly announced that she was running away from home. I guess she wanted to be free from such harsh treatment. She hurled open the front door and marched out in a scene reminiscent of a certain ten-year-old stomping out of a funeral home in Providence, Rhode Island. Apple and tree?

Debby paused at the street, looked back, looked up and down the quiet untraveled community lane, and appeared to be contemplating a critical issue. No runaway attempt can be successful without an act of defiance. So ignoring the clear rule of not stepping into, playing in, or crossing the street, Debby raced across the lane onto the opposite sidewalk. Clearly happy with her little four-year-old self, she strutted down the sidewalk past the neighbors' houses with her chest pumped out and her head held high. Two doors down, the resident family was in the yard working. The mother knelt in the flower bed, and the father and the children raked, hoed, and spread new loam to create a magnificent yard and garden. If you were a child, all you may have seen was dirt clumps and sweat. Debby stopped by the woman, watched for a few minutes, and then said, "I'm running away. May I come live with you?"

The mother, a quick and bright woman of Hispanic descent, did not miss a beat and said, "Of course, you can, honey, but if you live here, you must work. Everyone who lives here works." Debby looked at her, thought about it for a few moments, and then said, "No thanks" and headed on down the road. We didn't know what she was looking for. Maybe a family that wouldn't make her work or a family that would treat her like the princess she was. Who knows? The neighbor had seen us watching from the yard and knew that we were on top of this tableau as it unfolded. We were all grinning from ear to ear.

The sun began to set. Doris and I were back inside the house, peeking between the heavy drapes. Debby was standing on the sidewalk, contemplating her next move. She wasn't budging, and she was not coming home. Doris and I reviewed our options. I could just go across the street, snatch her up, and bring her home, but we rejected that one. I decided the solution was to send her sister out to convince her to come home. Julie was ten months younger than Debby and a dynamo herself. In a conspiratorial fashion, I enlisted our three-year-old daughter to go across the street and convince her sister to come home. On a scale of one to ten as solutions go, I thought I was off the charts.

Julie, with the confidence belying her young age, walked out the front door, gingerly made her way across the street and down the block. We could see the sisters in an animated discussion, but we couldn't hear their words. As if time was of the essence, Julie bolted back toward the house. Her arms and legs whipped back and forth, and she was flushed and highly excited. We too were excited, thinking Julie would arrive with manageable terms of surrender. She flipped open the front door and, not bothering to close it, raced upstairs. We were mystified, but not for long. Seconds later, Julie thundered back down the stairs with her bathing suit and a couple of pairs of underwear under her arm. As she leaped through the open front door, she announced, "I'm going with Debby." They weren't negotiating terms of surrender; they were forming a new alliance. Now I had two girls standing on the opposite sidewalk in the setting Texas sun debating their next move. On a scale of one to ten, maybe this idea was not off the charts after all—at least not off the high end.

Doris had had enough, and she saved the day. She proceeded down the block and informed the runaways that night was coming, dinner needed to be prepared, and she needed the girls' help. Doris said, "Come home, help me make dinner and set the table, and if you still want to run away later, you can." The three women in my life sauntered home, the bathing suits and underwear were refolded and stashed back in the bureau drawers, dinner was served, and the girls forgot they wanted to run away. Little did we know, this was a precursor of things to come.

We lived near a family of one of our returning prisoners of war. This man was of Japanese descent, and his family asked Doris to make a flower arrangement in his honor. Her training in Ikebana proved valuable. The arrangement was displayed at his homecoming and was so breathtaking it was photographed and shown in the San Antonio newspaper. The message in that arrangement may have been about the loss of innocence in war.

Chapter Nine

EXTERNAL SCARS

As I'm analyzing data, pruning roses, and chasing children down the street, I noticed a sore begin to develop on my face. It got worse with time and began to become red and irritated. The area just under my left eye began to swell and became painful. It appeared to be an open sore. Its small outline resembled a mini volcano nestled under the eye and against the nose. The edges were somewhat rounded with a concave center. I stopped by the clinic to have it looked at. The physician decided to do a biopsy on the sore, which he called a cyst. It felt a bit troubling, but I was under thirty, and things like that were treated like a hangnail.

A few days later, the biopsy was completed, the clinic called and asked if I would stop by to discuss the results. It was late June, and Doris and I were planning to celebrate our anniversary that weekend. So I said, "Sure, how about next week sometime?" The response came back, "How about two o'clock this afternoon?" Or in the language I'm used to, "Right now. This instant."

Welcome Home!

The sore or cyst turned out to be basal cell carcinoma, a form of skin cancer. This type of cyst manifested as a small sore on the surface of the face and had protrusions under the skin like tentacles that radiated out in all directions. The physicians diagrammed the lump for me, and it looked much like a spider. The concern was that continued growth of the cyst and tentacles could impact the eyes or the sinuses. Surgery was recommended immediately, right now, this instant, to remove the cancer.

The surgical procedure involved cutting out a swatch of my face around the cyst, ensuring the amount cut was somewhat larger than the cyst. The tissue removed from the face was sent to the pathology lab and examined to determine if the margins or edges of the piece of skin removed was free of cancer. I remained on the table with the wound open until the analysis was completed. If the chunk of me removed had no cancer on the edges, it was assumed they got it all. If the sample came back with cancer present in the tissue on the edges, then it was assumed the cut wasn't large enough. The surgeon would return to the operating room and remove more tissue, send it to the lab again, await results, and then repeat if necessary. After a few rounds of this, the hole in my face got bigger, my tolerance got lower, and everyone became edgy. I was looking up at the ceiling, afraid to turn to my left because I thought I would see a reflection of the man from Guam with no nose, but this time, it would be me. I was twenty-seven years old, and my face looked battered and beaten. The doctor finally gave the all-clear order, sewed me up, and sent me on my way.

Don't Hold Your Breath.

During a routine follow-up a few months later, a reoccurrence was diagnosed, and more surgery was required. I asked if we should have a plastic surgeon present since I was looking more and more like a Halloween mask as the days and surgeries progressed. In fact, during this time frame, I went to a birthday party in August, and someone told me I was two months early because Halloween wasn't until October. I went to a restaurant with some family members, and the waitress threw her hands over her face, saying, "Oh my god, I can't look." Mom was so angry she packed up the family and left the restaurant in search of an alternate diner that was a bit more compassionate. The surgeon's answer to the request for a plastic surgeon was, "Let's get rid of the cancer first, and then we'll call a plastic surgeon if necessary." The cutting continued.

I really couldn't blame people for their critical remarks. It looked horrible and only got worse. I don't remember exactly how many surgeries I underwent, but I estimate around twelve. This included the attempted repairs but did not include the additional cancerous spots found on my chest, back, and arms. The operation on my back left a huge hole. One day, someone asked if I had been shot. Thinking that was a more exciting story than the result of cancer, I contemplated saying yes! Of course, if I'd have been shot there, I wouldn't have been walking around to lie about it. I'd rather tell a lie than be bullied or made fun of even as an adult. In the case of my back, it was a joke and funny, but comparing my face to a Halloween mask was abusive.

Speculation began about the cause of this type of cancer not normally found in young people. It's an old man's disease, I was told. One obvious and probable option was a chemical called Agent Orange, an herbicide developed jointly by Great

Britain and the United States and first used in Malaysia by the British. In November 1961, President John F. Kennedy authorized the start of Operation Ranch Hand, the codename for the US Air Force's herbicide program in Vietnam. The program continued for ten years.

Kennedy authorized the use of this weapon to clear foliage around US bases. When the Viet Cong attacked bases in South Vietnam, they used the surrounding foliage to sneak up on the bases' perimeters. This allowed the enemy to get close to the runways or base entries before they could be spotted. Being close gave the VC a tactical advantage as they could launch a surprise attack from these positions. More injuries, more damage to the bases and aircraft were inflicted before the US defense force could respond and force the enemy to retreat. Normally, the enemy was beaten back, but this strategy significantly reduced the time our forces had to respond and defend themselves. The solution was to defoliate the forest in and around the bases by spraying the areas, called fogging, with Agent Orange. The defoliant was sprayed onto the forest by low-flying aircraft and killed all the vegetation it reached. Now we could see them coming.

Manufactured for the US Defense Department by Monsanto Corp. and Dow Chemical, Agent Orange got its name from the orange-striped barrels it was shipped in. It was the most widely used of the "Rainbow Herbicides" deployed during the war. Agent Orange contained an extremely toxic chemical called dioxin, a known human carcinogen. In some areas of Vietnam, the concentrations of dioxin in the soil and the water were hundreds of times greater than the levels considered safe by the US Environmental Protection Agency. But Agent Orange worked. Nothing was left standing or growing in the wake of the fogging, but once again, we didn't calculate the cost or assess the price we'd all have to pay. The decision to use Agent Orange left lasting effects on the troops who were exposed to it.

Agent Orange dumped on Yanks

WASHINGTON (AP)—Newly discovered military records indicate substantial numbers of GIs on military bases in Viet Nam were exposed to Agent Orange when planes on defoliation missions had to jettison their dangerous liquid cargo, the government said Wednesday.

"When I got this job . . . I didn't think anyone quite foresaw that we would be dumping this stuff on our own people (in Viet Nam)," Richard Schweiker, secretary of health and human services, said at a press conference.

Schweiker said Pentagon records showed 90 instances when airplanes dumped their chemical cargoes in emergencies, including 41 in which Agent Orange apparently was dumped "directly over or near U.S. air bases and other military installations."

THE NUMBER of men who came in contact with the spray "was substantially larger than anybody expected," he said. He could not estimate how many men that would be, he said.

Agent Orange contains dioxin, one of the most toxic chemicals in existence. About 60,000 Viet Nam veterans have told the Veterans Administration they fear their health was impaired by coming into contact with the chemical.

Some veterans blamed the herbicide for causing a vast variety of diseases—including cancer, birth defects in their children, miscarriages by their wives, impotency, respiratory problems, and liver, skin, nerve, and emotional disorders.

BUT SO FAR the VA has said it has no evidence that exposure causes any problem other than a skin disorder, and the VA has refused to pay disability compensation to veterans who blame their ailments on Agent Orange.

Schweiker said the Reagan administration had intensified efforts to examine the Pentagon's records.

"We didn't feel a high enough inquiry was made (previously)," he said.

He said it was not difficult to believe that crews on spraying missions would dump the herbicide near large groups of American troops because those missions had to end under emergency conditions—when the planes had been hit by enemy fire or their engines had failed.

SCHWEIKER SAID he was making the disclosure because he felt a responsibility "to really level with the American people with what really happened."

"We'd be glad to hear" from veterans who suspect they were exposed, he said.

Later, a department spokesman, declining to permit his name to be used, said veterans should write instead to the VA, which is compiling a registry of veterans who suspect exposure.

Schweiker said his department also is investigating reports that other American troops may have come into contact with the defoliant during base-clearing and river-bank spraying operations.

DURING THE WAR, 12 million gallons of Agent Orange were sprayed from planes to destroy food crops and jungle hiding places and clear vegetation from base camps, landing zones, waterways, and communications lines.

The spraying stopped in 1971 after Vietnamese women complained they were giving birth to high numbers of deformed babies as a result of coming into contact with the herbicide.

The Defense Department is now using that information to pinpoint the exact locations, times, weather conditions, the personnel present, and the extent of possible exposure, Schweiker's office said.

Until now, only some 1,200 pilots and support personnel who sprayed Agent Orange have been documented as having been heavily exposed to the defoliant.

Agent Orange

I spent many hours on the runway, awaiting replacement crews, waiting for repairs, and just waiting. The standard dress code during these waits was a flight suit unzipped to the waist with the top half lowered and tied around the waist, exposing the torso. This exposure may have resulted in my cancer. There has been no definitive cause and effect identified with the exposure to Agent Orange and skin cancer; however, there have been determinations that exposure to the defoliant contributed to other ailments.

The physical challenge has begun.

* * *

I looked at friends, family members, and even strangers passing by and thought, *Wow they've got it together. Look how good, how confident, how handsome they are. I wish I could be like them.* I may not even have known them. They could have been serial killers, psycho stalkers, or any number of deviant human beings; but I want to be like them. I compared my insides to their outsides. I couldn't see my outside, and I couldn't see their inside.

My looks and my image had been framed for me by the things Dad and others had said earlier in my life and the results of surgery. I was defined by the worst things I'd encountered or the worst things people said to me. I tried not to look at myself because I didn't want to see. I felt "less than," so anyone else looked good to me in comparison. What other people thought of me should be none of my business. What did I think of me? In my intellectual mind, I said, "Yeah, right, forget about them," but my heart echoed, "You're not enough." Now, not only was I not good enough, but I couldn't even look at myself in this condition.

Solutions continued to elude me, and I drank. At some point, I crossed the line, and I couldn't do without alcohol. I couldn't face a new dawn—I couldn't face a new job, a new world, or a new community. And most of all, I couldn't face a single individual.

On the outside, I lived life as if it was a scripted play. On the outside, I had a wife, three kids, the white picket fence (not the one in Nam), a job, family, friends, and all the trimmings a life should have. On the inside, the lights were dimming, and hope was ebbing. This was not the real me; it was someone else's reality. I was not engaged with myself. I was not the person I wanted to be. My heart was missing. In my heart, I abandoned the real me.

* * *

I decided to leave military service before they discovered my secret. My time was well before "don't ask, don't tell," and I knew my time was running out. Being in the middle of the face crisis was not an issue because the doctors told me I was "cured." So began the job hunt. I went to numerous job fairs and job interviews in the hopes of finding civilian employment that would start shortly after the Christmas holidays 1973. At twenty-eight, my face looked like I hit a brick wall at about eighty miles per hour. I had a bachelor of arts in psychology and limited experience in electronic warfare. I was labeled a "baby killer." What kind of work did I qualify for?

One weekend job fair in North Carolina was memorable because it landed me my first position. The fair took place in the ballroom of a hotel. Employers stood behind tables lined up against the outer walls, and the rows seemed to stretch forever. It felt like a meat market, and we were the ham hocks on display. An interview could be secured in one of two ways. First was by sending your résumé to a prospective employer in advance of the fair and securing a time slot. Or you could walk up to a table and hand them your résumé. They reviewed it in under thirty seconds, rendering a thumbs-up or thumbs-down. Since some of the employers didn't answer when a résumé was sent in advance, and since we didn't know every employer that was going to attend the fair, we often had to stand in line and endure the thirty-second appraisal. During the ten seconds after they read your résumé and began raising their heads to look you in the eyes and say no, you talked as fast as you could to convince them you were the answer to their hiring dreams.

Decisions were made on the spot. Most employers had two or three representatives conducting interviews simultaneously. If you passed the first thirty-second screening, you were scheduled for an additional interview later in the weekend, conducted in a saner environment in the hotel suite of that company's representatives. The job market had improved, and fifty or more employers looked for "the right fit" with a focus on returning vets. Even though hundreds of applicants attended, I felt like maybe I had a shot at this. It's not about I can't; I won the ribbon in the wrestling championship.

I had secured a few interviews in advance, and I approached other tables cold. One table I approached cold was manned by a team from Texas Instruments out of Dallas, Texas. They were opening a new manufacturing plant in Florida to produce a new line of electronic calculators, the SR-10 and SR-11. They were looking for first-line supervisors, and I thought maybe the electronics in my résumé would strike a resonant chord. After standing in line for a long time, I approached the table, handed a gentleman my résumé (stretched to fill one page with lots of open space and a big font), and waited. He spent the allotted thirty seconds reviewing the written words, handed me back my résumé, and said, "You're not what we're looking for. We need supervisors."

I said, "Yes, I know, and supervisors manage people. So my psychology education, my electronics training, and my leadership experience make me the perfect candidate for this job. Isn't it about motivating and understanding people?"

I have no idea where that confident response came from, but I had put on my little boy jacket and dared to cross that barren wasteland. Or maybe I was just aggravated at standing in line for what seemed like an eternity, and then in twenty to thirty seconds, this guy tells me to get lost—just like my high school football coach did. I was trying so hard to hang on to that spunky kid.

An interview was scheduled for later that evening. By the end of the interview, they said if I had my belongings in a U-Haul outside, I could start tomorrow. Was it my charm? Maybe they just thought I would scare employees into behaving because I looked so bad. My discharge from the Navy was slated for later in December, and we agreed my start date in Florida would be right after the New Year. I was offered eleven thousand dollars a year to start, and I was elated.

Our plan was to travel by car from San Antonio, Texas to Bradford, Pennsylvania, located in the northwestern corner of Pennsylvania. I wanted to visit family before starting the new job. After the holidays, we would jump back in the car and move to Fort Walton Beach, Florida, and begin a new chapter of our lives.

Once the decision was made to leave the service, it was important to the Navy that I be declared cancer-free. Not being cancer-free, not being in the same condition as I was in when I entered the service, might mean a disability and long-term care. A few weeks before my discharge, I noticed my face was not healing. My last surgery a month or so prior was supposed to be healed and done with. Instead, it looked swollen, red, and black and blue. I went to the clinic for an examination and was told everything was fine. Just the normal healing process, they assured me. All was supposedly in order, so we packed out and loaded up the station wagon. With the wife, three kids, one dog, and tons of luggage in tow, we began the trek north. We were all excited for Christmas at home and then on to a new life in Florida. The trip was scheduled for about two and half days because we didn't want to push it with the kids.

So Much for Not Pushing It

My face kept getting bigger and bigger and blacker and blacker as blood filled the cheek. It was extremely painful. I was trying to continue in the driver's seat and not put any more pressure on Doris. She had her hands full with the kids. We stopped for gas in St. Louis, and as I pumped the fuel, my face erupted. The profuse bleeding scared a few people, including myself. I drove on with a handkerchief pressed to my face, but nothing staunched the bleeding. Locating a pay phone, I called Dad and said I'm in trouble. I told him what was happening and advised him we were not stopping for the night but beelining it to Bradford—included in the call was the urgent request to see a doctor ASAP. We arrived in Bradford near midnight. Small-town USA had its advantages. We were met in the driveway by Dad and a local doctor. I could always count on Dad in an emergency.

The doctor gave me the once over, then gave Dad a look over my shoulder that can only be described as, "Oh shit." Hoping I didn't notice the look, they moved me immediately to Dad's car and off to the hospital. The family was hustled into the house, exhausted and worried. It had been another trip from hell. The physician examined my face and declared, "You need surgery." I said okay and suggested we wait until after Christmas. He said, "No, now." Why does everyone in my life always have to say *now*?

The surgery was described as a facial labial fold or nasolabial surgery. Not to be confused with the labia. That could have been embarrassing. The surgeon cut from the outside edge of my left eye near the ear, then under the eye all the way to my nose and almost down to the lips. He then pulled back the flap and removed much of the cheek tissue. When he was done, the cheek and its loose flap looked like an earmuff that had gone catawampus on my face. After the surgeon sewed the flap back in place, I was beat to the bone. My face was hideous before, now there were no words for the ugly that followed that procedure. Many of the muscles and nerves in my face were severed, so the left side drooped like the boobs of my coworker, Evelyn, in the pill-packing plant.

An unexpected battle began with the Veterans Administration. The VA refused to pay for the operation, the hospital stay, and the required follow-up treatment. They admonished me for having the surgery in a civilian hospital. Located just fifty miles away in Erie, Pennsylvania was a VA facility. Apparently, the plan should have been to travel the fifty miles over mountainous terrain in the middle of winter, holding my face on to have the surgery there. Ignorance of the rule or not, fifty more miles was out of the question.

The VA eventually paid. During the dispute, all my medical records were reviewed. The bad news revealed in the reports of the original surgery included the finding that cancer was present in the margins of the sample of skin taken from my cheek. The procedure should have been to take a wider swatch of skin and keep cutting until the reports read all clear. Apparently, they just threw in the towel, closed the wound, and sent me on my way.

My face wasn't clear of cancer, and the saga continued. Now there wasn't much face left. The current dilemma, with limited meat on my face, was how to take more, ensure the cancer was gone, and sew it up again. The next surgery included removing a section of the cheek in the corner between the nose and the eye. With nothing to sew back down on the front of the face, the doctor took a skin graft from the flesh behind my ear. I wondered why they didn't take a hunk off my fat ass. From what I was told, there was plenty to spare.

That surgery was so painful. I threw one of the surgeons out of the operating room. He wouldn't listen, and whatever he was doing wasn't working for me. The pain was like an intense, continuous sting of a giant bee. It didn't stop, and I kept saying I can feel that, and it got worse every time he touched me. The lead surgeon nodded at the second doctor, and he left quietly.

A second spot had been discovered on my chin, diagnosed positive, and removed successfully during this time frame. By the 1980s, there were no more reoccurrences and no more surgeries on the face. The cancer was under control, but I looked like a Picasso painting. The VA hospital in Phoenix, Arizona, cared for me now, and I received excellent support. The primary doctor responsible for my care was a dermatologist named Helen. One day, she looked at my droopy and scarred-torn face and said, "I bet we can fix that." She contacted a plastic surgeon from the nearby Indian Health Service hospital and asked him to look at my face. He turned out to be a miracle worker on deformities of the face.

Most of my surgeries had resulted in a cut from the eye southward toward the lip that caused a wide scar along my nose despite the fact they had bandaged and tied my face together like it was dry cleaning. The plastic surgeon, convinced he could fix my face, said hop on the table. Being awake, wide-eyed, and bushy-tailed for most of these adventures turned out to be a necessity. The surgeons needed to see my wrinkles, laugh lines, and the symmetry of my face. There weren't many laugh lines anymore. This wasn't funny. The surgeon started in on the abused and tired face, cutting horizontally under the nose and out toward the cheek, lifting the drooping face. That cut turned the upper lip up and out. A second cut, on the inside of my mouth, corrected that anomaly, and the lip was flipped down and tucked back into place. I'm sure there was more to it, but that's all I remember him saying. When he was done, he stood me up. I looked in the mirror, and I began silently crying. I knew it was over. I knew with the end of the healing I wouldn't scare little kids anymore.

* * *

A few years after this surgery, I moved to San Diego, and my follow-up care continued. The VA was concerned about the residual scarring and put my case before a panel. Doctors from the Mayo Clinic, the University of California, San Diego, the VA, and a local physician discussed possible options. We sat around a conference table, brainstorming options like derm-abrasion, collagen treatments, more surgery, and things beyond me. After listening patiently for a long time, I stood, pushing my chair away from the table. The scraping of the metal chair legs on the tile floor made everyone look my way. I stood and said, "Thank you, but there won't be any more procedures. I'm happy with the way my face looks." Elated and walking on air, I left the conference. Eventually, my face healed to the point no one noticed the scars. My journey took me from being an apparition that forced people to look away to speaking in front of small and large groups across the United States.

One convention gave me the opportunity to speak in front of fifteen hundred people. The engagements where memora-ble, and I performed with confidence and comfort. One smaller group was a convention for Women in Cable TV. I was the keynote luncheon speaker discussing alcohol and drugs in the workplace. The audience extended the conversation from the workplace to the home, and it touched many families on a per-sonal level. The ladies kept asking me questions and telling me to go on. Finally, the vice president of a local communications company, responsible for the program, intervened and ended the presentation. The applause was over-the-top.

Chapter Ten

INTERNAL SCARS

The Insides May Be More Difficult to Fix

I was trying to be the hero, the leading man, and I didn't even know who I was or what role to play. I survived Vietnam. I survived dozens of surgeries, but I wanted to die. I worked hard, and the feelings didn't go away. I tried to be a good husband and father, and nothing changed. I drank, and nothing changed.

I couldn't tell anyone, and I couldn't keep it a secret. There was too much hidden inside—so much I wanted to share. I couldn't tell any friends about the war, I couldn't tell those close to me about my pains, and above all, I couldn't tell a soul about my loves. My experiences in this world had shown there was little concern for the dignity and respect of others and little to no acceptance of differences. It was to get worse. No amount of accomplishments—no success quotient could offset the feeling of failing.

I was not enough, to begin with, I was not enough now, and if anyone knew I was gay, the discussion on my worth would end—unfavorably. I was not the son, the brother, the husband, and the father I wanted to be because I'm gay.

The real reason I didn't feel loved and wanted is because I didn't love or want to be me. I shrank my world to a day, a minute, maybe this second so I could manage my secrets of war and love and not slip up. I limited who I saw, what I did, and where I went to avoid leaving a trail of clues. No one must ever find out.

Breaking Point

I did not think a lot about suicide between the ages of twenty and twenty-five because it felt like everyone around me wanted to do it for me. I was in training, flying in old planes, and in Vietnam fighting to not die. I came home, and I didn't want to go on. It was exhausting. I was so tired. I was dealing with the memories, the sights and sounds of war, multiple surgeries, alcohol use, transitioning from the military to civilian life, and loving men. None of this makes sense.

There was no transition back and, therefore, no home for me. I felt safer in a war zone than alone on Main Street, USA. I spent two years at the Air Force Special Forces Communication Center in San Antonio, Texas, with eight other Navy men, and I don't remember a thing about them. I have a vague recollection of the leader who was a large man with dark hair and dark glasses, but nothing other than that. I don't believe they were ever *in-country*, and they couldn't relate. They didn't even know what to ask. I'm sure they never knew I was troubled, and if they were troubled in any way, I didn't know it. We never spoke about our aloneness.

Men who served in Vietnam and returned home seemed to disperse into the ether. I never saw and didn't speak to another veteran of that conflict. I was alone in a crowd and drowning on dryland. It's hard to share with someone who's never been there or done that. I wasn't looking for answers just a nod, a grunt of acceptance or understanding. Just a safe place to breathe. Just a place in this world for me. It really didn't seem like much to ask, but I just couldn't get a grip, a foothold, or a lifeline.

* * *

The job I landed with Texas Instruments abruptly ended in 1975. My gainful employment of one year, as a frontline supervisor making the first line of electronic calculators for Texas Instruments (TI), had been an exciting year. These state-of-the-art calculators, called the SR-10 and SR-11, were mass produced in the Fort Walton Beach facility. My assembly line, primarily women, were the top of the line. We worked hard, laughed, and made our employer successful. We outproduced most other lines on any given day. We ran hard, partied together, and developed a team spirit unsurpassed to this day. Unfortunately, the team spirit quality isn't a measurable metric, and the good times ended.

The semiconductor crisis and economic downturn of the early seventies hit like the rockets of Vietnam. TI's headquarters in Texas let word leak that the Florida division would be closing, and all the work transferred to facilities in the Dallas area. The Dallas market was stable, and TI didn't want to be the odd man out by laying off a bunch of people in the Dallas / Fort Worth area. My bosses assured me, based on my performance, of a transfer to Dallas. When the big day came, I was laid off with everyone else. The C-level executive decided that any employee transferred from Dallas to Fort Walton would be retained and moved back to Dallas. Those hired specifically for Florida would be laid off—neat, clean, legal, and done.

Welcome to Unemployment

We moved to Mississippi. The only option for a war-torn (literally), unemployed, alcoholic, gay husband and father of three with half a face.

After an extensive job-search tour up and down the East Coast, we found ourselves in Tunica, Mississippi. Now if God were going to give the world an enema in the midseventies, he would have stuck it in Tunica. Job fairs in Miami, Atlanta, Washington, DC, and interviewing with many companies produced no options. Then Tunica called. Graceland was less than an hour north, and desperately, I tried to hear Elvis sing "Follow That Dream." No luck.

My interview in Tunica for the job as assistant plant manager of a textile manufacturer was successful. Good fortune had smiled on me, and the job was offered on the spot. Accepting the job and starting immediately impressed the owners. They marveled at my flexibility and reliability. If the truth were to be told, it wasn't flexibility or reliability that prompted me to accept on the spot; it was lack of funds. There was no money to go back to Florida and get the family. They were staying near Disney World with Gary and Judy, our former neighbors on Guam. When we moved out of our house in Fort Walton Beach with no firm destination in mind, we took the kids to Disney World.

Affording the Disney excursion was taxing and wandering around the park, with three children and our friends, caused my anxious mind to drift. Suddenly I heard Doris say, "Have you got the baby?" I looked down, and he was gone. Getting immediately defensive, my retort was, "I thought you had him."

We began looking, believing he couldn't have gotten far. At first, we could not find him or see him in the sea of tourist. My yelling and running in one direction, and Doris and our friends headed in other directions produced no results. Panic set it, and it was too reminiscent of the feelings from Vietnam. That all-consuming feeling of powerlessness and doom. My insides tightened, I couldn't breathe, and my heart raced at a frantic pace.

Then about one hundred yards away, I spotted Matt headed for the pink elephants of the Dumbo ride. He was "hell-bent for leather," not even noticing his parents were lost. Matt, not acclimated to the mechanics of the park, headed toward the back of the ride. The ticket agent, loading tiny passengers on the elephants at the front of the ride, did not see him. The agent strapped the last rider on the plastic pachyderm and moved toward the control panel to start the ride. Matt had reached his pink destination and began to climb up on one of the stationary animals. Like a slow-motion film, the agent moved toward the start button, Matt climbed, and the fifty yards between me and the musical beasts did not bode well for a happy ending. I began running, as if eluding rockets, and screaming at the top of my lungs for the operator to keep the switch in the "off" position. It sounded more like, "NO, NO, NO…"

He could not hear me over the din of the crowd. The new world record for the fifty-yard dash was accomplished that day. With a final leap and grab, I snatched Matt off the back of that prickly pink elephant and collapsed safely a few feet away. The annoying music played, the elephants went up and down, from side to side, and Matt did not understand the commotion. He also didn't understand why no one got on that ride that day.

We'll Blame the Elephants

Getting Doris and the kids from Florida to Tunica with our few meager possessions required a loan of $500 from my brother.

Tunica is a small town in the northwest corner of Mississippi near the Mississippi River. At the time, this rural town was one of the most impoverished places in the United States. It was semifamous for the particularly deprived neighborhood known as "Sugar Ditch Alley," named for the open sewer located there. Its fortunes have improved since development of a gambling resort nearby. I hope the treatment of the residents has improved as well.

The factory was owned by New Yorkers, so the contrast of ideologies was a challenge. The New Yorkers wanted to save every nickel they could, and yet they had to be seen favorably by the local wealthy white population of cotton farmers.

Confusion set in during my first plant tour when cool blasts of air hit me forcefully in certain spots, and then extreme heat and humidity were prevalent in other areas. Sometimes this dichotomy occurred in the same room. When I questioned the plant manager about the air irregularities, he called it "spot air-conditioning." The spot where a white supervisor stood had bursts of cool refreshing air and where the predominately black workforce had to spend most of their day there was no air.

The place was dirty, smelly, and just plain nasty. Many employees chewed tobacco and spit the wads into open spittoons or coffee cans. They aimed for these receptacles but often missed. The textiles manufactured there were mattress pads and other bedding products. Once when reviewing a customer return, a big wad of chewed tobacco was found in the middle of the folded material. Not something you wanted to rest on. I had to revisit and revise my assessment that good fortune had smiled down on me.

The town was very small, and no housing was available when we arrived, so we rented an apartment on the south side of Memphis. From there, I thought I heard Elvis singing, "In the Ghetto." Eventually, a small two-bedroom house became available in town. We were not number one on the list of prospective renters, but because of the stature of being the *white* assistant plant manager and the influence of those connected to the plant, we got the place. I had power just because of my skin color.

Prior to our move in, we ordered a washer and dryer from the local appliance store. The walk through the downtown square on my way to the appliance dealer alarmed me. I saw two water fountains; one had a sign on it that said whites only, and the other one said blacks. The ordered washer and dryer were promptly delivered even though I signed nothing, paid nothing, and provided no background information. Eventually, the items were paid, but that seemed odd. They knew where to find me, literally, and I was white. Plus they knew the owner of the plant would see it to it they were taken care of if I welched on the unspoken, unsigned deal.

Welcome to the Old South, Circa 1975

The house was small, old, and quaint in a village sort of way, but it was warped. The heat and the humidity warped the house. We put a wood and marble coffee table we purchased in Taiwan on the living room floor, and it rocked. It literally rocked up and down. My beer would wash back and forth in the glass like a small wave when any one of the kids leaned on the table.

For the move from Memphis to Tunica, my employer sent a truck with three or four men. He wanted it done quickly—like now, this instant. Doris went on ahead to the new house with the children and prepared a lunch for the moving crew. The lunch fit for kings, spread out on tablecloths on the front porch looked amazing. I was starved, and I knew my associates were too.

When the men saw the feast on the porch, they hung their heads low and looked away. They immediately began to unload the truck. I interrupted their efforts and said, "Break time. Come on over and eat." The men stood off a few feet and refused to approach the porch. I had to aggressively interrogate them to learn what was wrong. "Don't you like the food? Is it cold? Not cooked the right way? What's up?" They were starved, and I knew it.

Finally, one man got up the nerve to tell me that they could not eat on my front porch because they were black, and that wasn't allowed. I initially refused to accept that and said, "It's my porch, and you're my guests, and you're helping me. Please come sit." All the men vehemently shook their heads and loudly said no. The repercussions for violating that rule outweighed starving. Finally, they relented a bit and said if we moved the food to the *back* porch, they could join us.

We moved the food to the back porch, and immediately, everyone launched into the lunch. They were starving. What a way to live.

Not My Kinda Town

The house was old and needed painting. The electrical sockets were old and unprotected. Everything was old. One day, Doris and I were sitting on the couch watching the coffee table rock when we heard a loud unfamiliar pop. Immediately after the pop, the baby rolled by like a beach ball. Matthew had stuck a bobby pin in an electrical socket and was sent on a shocking tour of the new place. His hand had a black scorch mark, mirroring a bobby pin etched on it.

It wasn't his last inquisitive adventure by any means. He constantly inspected, disassembled, and tried to understand the mechanics of everything in sight. The difficult part of that trait was that he couldn't put anything back together again, and worse, neither could his father.

The place, dull and drab, needed a bit of sprucing up. Painting the exterior would make everything more pleasing. The house wasn't that big. We could do this, especially since the girls, six and seven years old, wanted to help. I failed to calculate the effects of the heat and humidity. Day 2, Daddy's on the ladder, the girls below and the perfect little painter's assistants, looked up to see the lead painter do a header on the grass. Initially, they laughed, applauded, and said, "Do it again, Daddy!" When I didn't respond, didn't even move, they didn't know whether to laugh or cry. They screamed for Mommy and tried to relay that Daddy had just done a swan dive onto the grass and was not moving.

I remember becoming a little dizzy, and I must have momentarily passed out. Later, when fully conscious, I planned to get right back to my painting. I just couldn't do it. I was weak, woozy, and I had an earache. This event caused me to make my first trip to a doctor's office in our new town.

The physician selection process was easy. There was only one doctor in town. No appointments needed; walk-ins welcomed. Entering the front door of the office created immediate confusion. A partition, in the middle of the room, extended from the front door to the reception counter. A waiting room on the left contained cheap chairs, a cheap coffee table, which didn't rock, old magazines, and a reception desk with a window. A mirror image of this waiting room appeared on the right. No signs, no notes, and no directions were visible. Maybe there were two doctors in this office. I flipped a coin, turned left, and walked to the counter. On the reception counter was an old fashion bell. To ring the bell, you had to slap your palm on the top, depressing the ringer against the domed cover. Gently, my palm glided over the top of bell and summoned help. Nurse

Cratchit came from the back and looked at me like I was covered in mold. In a pinched voice, she informed me I was on the wrong side of the partition. The left side was for blacks. How could I be so stupid?

No one was on either side, which prompted me to just launch into the reason for my visit. Nurse C. refused to serve me. She moved to the other reception window, stood there, and waited for me to come around the partition. Arriving on the "white side," my mouth opened to introduce myself and my problem, and she interrupted me to tell me who I was and why I was there. She already knew even though she had never laid eyes on me before that moment. I think the news of my swan dive off the ladder had already reached her.

Small-Town USA in the South

After a thorough and complete exam, especially of the ears, the doctor told me to stop swimming. Living near the Mississippi River must have given him the idea that I swam often. I had never, nor will I ever, go into that body of water, and there was no pool in my backyard. I told the physician that I hadn't been underwater in years. I don't even take baths. After seeing the panicked look on his face, I quickly added, "I take showers instead of baths." The doctor said I had swimmer's ear. Sweat caused by the heat, and humidity of that region created my swimmer's ear.

Thus far, Tunica and I were not embracing each other. As usual, I drank a bit and went to work hungover. Being hungover and faced with a hot, humid, and stinky place to work was not a winning combination. The factory smelled of sweat, tobacco, oil, and fiber. My symptoms, resembling morning sickness, lasted for almost a year. It wasn't just the physical environment that made me ill; it was the way people were treated.

One morning, an older white female supervisor stood with me as we assessed the operations. A young black female walked by, carrying a coffee can, a clean one, and asked for a donation. In response to my inquiry, she told me a coworker had lost her trailer, and all her possessions in a fire the previous evening, and they were trying to help. I reached into my pocket, pulled out a few bills, and placed them in the coffee can. She thanked me profusely and moved on. I heard muttering to my left, and when I looked toward the white female supervisor, she hissed, "She's got some nerve." The supervisor was appalled that this employee had the nerve to approach white folks and ask for a handout. The supervisor's hands never left her apron pockets to help in any way.

Another instance of confusion arose when a new black lady appeared on the line, folding mattress pads. I asked the supervisor who the new employee was and how she got there. Hiring was my responsibility and I hadn't been involved in any interviews with this woman. The supervisor informed me that the woman worked for one of the farm owners, and she was pregnant. After seeing my dumbfounded look, she went on to explain the lady needed to be covered by the medical benefits provided by this workplace for her delivery. As soon as she delivered, she'd be fired from here and sent back to the fields. This was a regular practice and an arrangement made by the owners with the Southern Gentry of the area.

The bigotry didn't just focus on skin color; it was male and female as well. Once, and only once, we were invited to an elegant party at one of the farms. We were excited to see the beautiful antebellum mansion and the antique furnishings. Doris and I meandered up the long walkway, admiring the landscape, the wraparound porches, the beautiful white-painted columns gracing the entrance, and proceeded inside. Delicate finger foods were served by the servants as we mingled. We wandered into a crowded living space and only saw men. In an adjacent room, we stumbled on all the women. They completely separated by gender. At first, I hung with the men as I tried to assimilate to the culture, but I soon became bored and wandered into the other room seeking my wife.

The other women looked at me like my fly was open and parts unmentionable were visible. Eventually, the hostess came over and politely informed me that the men were in the smoking parlor. I said, "Yeah, I know, but I want to be with my wife." We were never invited back. In fact, we were never invited to another party in that town, and I know there were many.

Follow the rules or get out.

Chapter Eleven

GO WEST

Eleven months after we arrived in Tunica, I got a call from Phoenix, Arizona. Sperry Flight Systems had my résumé from one of the job fairs I attended after the Texas Instrument plant closed. I was not in an active job search at that time. Eleven months it took them to call me. What took so long? Of course, I'll come to Arizona. Just get me out of here.

I flew to Arizona and interviewed for a front-line supervisor position. The offer had a starting salary of $11,000 per year. We were making bank again. I let them know that I'd take any job. I didn't really care; we were on our way. That's how bad it was.

In the mid to late seventies, Corporate America was experimenting with team building programs. Sperry Flight Systems was on board with this concept. They wanted to develop leaders and to work in teams based on skill sets, not color or gender. I was hired for one specific position, then rotated through many.

Unfortunately, the brown desert of Arizona reminded me of Vietnam, except for the Christmas lights wrapped around the cacti. Fortunately, the rice paddies were replaced with Camelback Mountain and South Mountain. The sun rose and set majestically, casting shadows, and creating colors I didn't know existed. Then summer came.

Welcome to the Wild West

I was first assigned as a supervisor for the assembly of flight controls. In this role, I learned to walk the tightrope between the company's needs and representing the employees. I took a stand supporting one employee's work when it was challenged and won that battle for her. The employee looked at me with a look of gratitude and appeared speechless. She said no one ever stood up for her like that before. We made a difference.

My second position was as a production planner on the space shuttle program. Sperry was working on a component of the communication link to the shuttle. I was invited to go to the NASA launch site, Kennedy Space Center, at the USAF Base Cape Canaveral and observe a space shuttle launch, and it was awe-inspiring in more ways than one.

While in Florida, I sneaked away to Daytona Beach and finally visited my first gay bar. I drank, danced, and was intimate with a man. I couldn't believe I did it, and I was terrified. The guy seemed to be attracted to me and wanted to see me again. I said yes but really didn't want to see him again. I thought he might come looking for me or worse someone might discover what I was doing. I really didn't want that reality. I checked out of my hotel room the next morning and flew back to Phoenix days early. I got so drunk I had to be escorted off the plane because I couldn't find my ticket, my briefcase, or anything. I couldn't even remember where I was supposed to be going.

The Truth Was, I Wasn't Going Anywhere

Upon my return from Florida, Sperry selected me to become the manager of the maintenance department. I used the same psychology argument about working with people that had worked with Texas Instruments. It worked again. The question then loomed: Can a nontechnical person lead a technical team? I had a degree in psychology and could not put the stuff back together that my son disassembled.

The facility in the North Phoenix area had state of the art 1970s equipment, clean rooms, and much more. My toughest challenge turned out to be my employees. Technicians would give me bad information or get way too technical, knowing it flew over my head. My total technical expertise consisted of knowing if the on-off switch was in the "on" or "off" position. I ended those games by clearly stating what I knew and what I didn't know. I pointed out that my job was not to repair the machinery but to provide support and management for the team. Their job was to fix stuff. If we all did our jobs and worked together and stopped with the games, we'd create a win-win situation. And we did.

The facilities department and the maintenance department were archenemies at that time. Each blamed the other for failures. There was no communication between the two departments, and the leaders couldn't be in the same room for more than two minutes without arguing. Working in concert with the facilities manager, that atmosphere changed. We worked together, and the plant ran smoothly. What I lacked in technical skills was offset by my counterpart in facilities. He helped me with those issues, and I coached him on the softer management and employee relations challenges. We worked as a team and made it happen.

From the technical front, I moved into employee relations. I didn't have to deal with some of the same issues that faced me in Tunica, but new issues arose. Gender identity, sexual orientation and harassment conflicts began to surface in the workplace. Many people were just as bigoted about these struggles. I traded race and gender discrimination in Tunica for sexual orientation and gender issues. In the 1970s, we had only two genders and closed minds.

The initial gender identity crisis erupted in a storm. Women of the workforce marched into my office in the heat of rebellion, demanding that I make "that" person use the men's room. "That" person was eventually identified as a man in the process of changing his gender. Still in transition, Paul presented as male, not female. That was the problem. In my discussions with the women, they expressed their discomfort and discontent with a man using the same bathroom. Paul, soon to be Colleen, insisted she had to use the women's restroom. He was planning and preparing for surgery. Candidates for this surgery were required to live for a year prior to the operation as a person of the gender they most identified with and who they would become after surgery. For Paul, that was female.

We compromised and found a locked restroom not frequented by the rebellious crowd and Paul, a.k.a. Colleen, was given the key to use as she saw fit. Comfort for all. Separate but equal. Don't ask, don't tell, long before the Clinton compromise and still not right.

The second issue arose when a young man of twenty-three stormed into my office irate that a person of the same sex was stalking him and asking him out. He showed me a love note recently passed to him by the smitten coworker. He was outraged. Imagine someone interested in an extremely handsome, fit young tanned Arizona cowboy? What's this world coming to?

I called the "stalker" into my office to discuss the issue, absolutely assured in my own mind that the "perp" would deny any wrongdoing. I was utterly amazed when I confronted him with his latest love letter. This hallmark advance included an invitation to go out on a dinner date. I asked him if he wrote the romantic overture, as it was unsigned. He said, "Oh yes, that's me, and I hope he says yes this time."

This Time

I inquired as to how his love interest responded to his previous approaches, and the gentleman responded, "Man, did he get angry. I don't understand why this upsets him so much. He went ballistic. It doesn't make sense to me. I just want to go out with him."

The way forward for this case was clearly defined. I began the coaching lesson with "no means no." No does not mean not at this moment, ask again later. No is not a teasing gesture demanding you continue your advances. No is not an indication that *I'm confused, and you know better.* No means don't ask again. Just as with any romantic approach, when someone says no, they mean no, and you are to stop asking. Further approaches will be viewed as harassment and are inappropriate anywhere, especially in the workplace.

The suitor was full of remorse and regret but agreed that he would not pursue the young man again. I think the remorse and regret were not for the reasons I hoped for. He was warned that if he did pursue this man again, he was subject to discipline up to and including termination. The issue wasn't same sex or opposite sex; it's treating others with dignity and respect.

I was promoted to the manager of the employee relations department and led the efforts to resolve problems like these for this workforce of approximately three thousand men and women. I loved it.

Let Me Look at Their Problems and Not Mine

I remained in the field for the next forty years. I continued my studies, earned a master's degree in human resource management, and consulted with many different companies to create a culture that works, a culture that cares and a culture that generates profit. These are not mutually exclusive goals.

Chapter Twelve

DEADLY SILENCE

Welcome to Denial, and It Ain't a River Somewhere

I tried to carry on, but the weight of my secret became unbearable, and the drinking was alcoholic. I drank every day and every night. I had my drink when there is no milk in the refrigerator for the kids. I drank for the strength to go on and to forget and to keep me on the straight and narrow, and I do mean straight. I drank to shrink my world and create routines that hid the essence of me. Most importantly, I drank because I'm an alcoholic.

I have the disease of alcoholism, and it runs deep in my family. I drank beer. Yes, I'm a garden variety drunk, and drinking beer like I did was alcoholic. Alcohol was my drug of choice, and if it did not do for me what I wanted it to do, I would have found another drug.

It worked from the first double date with Brother Bill until 1976 when it turned on me. That was a hell like no other. No matter how much I drank, I could not change me. I wanted to numb the pain. If any joy or happiness was present in my life, I didn't notice. Like watching the old black-and-white TV in the house in Rhode Island. No color and sheer terror. I was seven again, and I want to put on my jacket and go find someone to hold my hand and make me feel safe.

I drank when I was happy. I drank when I was sad. I drank to celebrate the opening of a new pack of cigarettes. It didn't matter. I just drank so I didn't have to face the reality of me.

There are many ways to commit suicide. You can do it quickly with a gun or slowly by drinking yourself to death, and I was on the latter path. Bertrand Russell said drunkenness is temporary suicide. I was contemplating making it permanent.

After all, it was a struggle to get up, dress, open the door, and go for groceries. It took effort to be on full alert for the next attack. It took so much energy to look in front, in back, and on both sides. To look above and below. To see, to hear, and to be ready for what might come next. Worse than the next attack was the fear of discovery. Did they see me? Did they know? It seemed more painful in my mind to say this is really who I am. To tell you I've been living a lie for thirty years. Yet how could that be more painful than what I was feeling and experiencing every day? I was tired. Even if I tried, even if I showed the courage to say, "See me, see me as I am" would those who mattered accept me?

The world I had experienced to date and the lessons life taught me would lead to a resounding negative answer on that last question. My country sent me off to fight a war no one wanted, and I never came home. Women were treated as less than and relegated to the home. People of color were treated as outcasts and servants, and we didn't dare utter the word gay. If we did utter a reference to homosexuality, it was by tying the offending party to a fence and beating them to death. There appeared to be no room for differences and no chance for acceptance of any sort. No one was even there to talk about it, and I thought I was safe in silence.

Welcome to Silence That Can Kill

The family reunions continued, and shortly after I returned from the Far East, we had a reunion in Hudson, Ohio. I flew there alone and walked in to be greeted by the usual family crowd. I heard laughing, and multiple conversations going on at the same time. I heard children playing and getting reacquainted with cousins, and I smelled the aromas from the kitchen. I wanted to rekindle the memories from before, but I felt like an outsider. I was not the person in that iconic photo. Maybe Mom was right when she said, "He may not make it home."

I lasted just over a day at the reunion. By early day 2, I was in the guest bedroom lying on the floor between the bed and the wall, talking on the phone to the airline reservation desk and asking for the next flight out. Unfortunately, that didn't work, and I had to gut out the next day or two. I was in a crowd, and I could not have been more miserable or alone. A crowd of family that loved me. I couldn't feel it. I couldn't relate or reintegrate even into my own family.

* * *

I could handle the war, the memories, and the sounds. What I couldn't handle was the sound of silence. I shrunk my world until it didn't matter anymore. I avoided contact with other people and other situations to remain hidden. I put one foot in front of the other and did the bare minimum to survive. And it backfired. With a world so small and devoid of emotion, what did I have to lose? It would take only one small step to leave such a small world. The pain would stop, and what had I given up? Just a small, dark, and lonely world that was not much to enjoy.

Like Skip said in the EC-121, I got this crisis covered, but if anything else went wrong, we were screwed. What if I garnered enough courage to come out and found myself alone again? What if I told my war stories and was still called a baby killer? What if I got plastic surgery and everyone still looked away? What if I checked the locks on the door and someone broke into the house?

Chapter Thirteen

THE DAY BEFORE

Welcome to the Way Forward and the Way Home

Confusion reigned and conflict bit like a pool of piranha. I thought of suicide every day. As my thoughts contemplated that solution, it grew stronger day by day. I was convincing myself that was the answer. I weighted different options on how to do it. I didn't want to create problems for my family, so it had to be neat and clean. This ending frightened me, but the thought of a future of conflict and confusion was more intimidating. Was this to be the end?

I wanted to change the ending. The end would need to be redefined as the end to misery, the end to conflict, and eventually, the end to seeing suicide as an option. Was there enough time to change the ending? I was not sure. It doesn't feel that way. It felt like the day before I died.

* * *

I met a man in Phoenix, and my life as I knew it ended again. As I was contemplating suicide, the reality of me came alive in the arms of Sebastian.

When I was with Sebastian, I felt safe. I realized I had longed to feel safe. I longed for comfort and to find a place for me in this world. Had I found it? I felt blood coursing through my veins and could feel the power of me. I felt alive for the first time in a long time, and I thought, *Now here's something that could give me the will to go on.* I believed I could tell him everything and not be judged and rejected. I wanted him in my life, and I didn't know how to make that work. Confusion had narrowed my perception, and pain blotted out most of what was defined as my world, and maybe it wasn't that small after all. Doubt crept in between comfort and hope; having a wife, three kids, and a boyfriend didn't seem like an equation destined to succeed in the late seventies.

We dated secretly for about six months, and desperation grew. I couldn't reconcile what was happening, and I couldn't deny my reaction to it. While in high school and college, I had an experience or two with the same sex, but I thought it was a phase I was going through or an experiment. This was no experiment now, and there was no denying the truth anymore. Initially, the conflict increased, and pain hit new heights. Not believing there was an answer, the desire to take that small step from my darkness to my demise seemed attractive, easy, and simple. Suicide was the easier, softer way.

Hope for Another Solution

When Sebastian and I went out to dinner, I noticed he didn't drink at all. I found that weird. I asked him why. He told me he had a problem with drinking in the past, but he was now sober. He attended a twelve-step program, and that helped him quit and find a new way to live. I thought, *Nice for you, but not for me.*

In February of 1977, he asked me to attend one of his meetings. I thought I'd go just to be supportive of his problem, not because I needed help. During the meeting, a film was shown featuring a well-known priest talking about the disease of alcoholism. In one segment, the priest said, "I was working at a radio station in Alaska, and at midnight, this guy calls and says, 'I drink two six-packs of beer every night. Am I an alcoholic?'" I sat there wondering if I had ever called a radio station in Alaska at midnight? I left the auditorium at the break and walked around the parking lot, wondering aloud. Sebastian came out to see if I was okay. I asked him if he thought I was an alcoholic. He said, "Only you can answer that question." Thanks for your help, but also thanks for letting me off the hook.

I Can't Live As I Am, I Can't Live As You Do, and I'm Not Giving Up My Alcohol?

My small world was glued together by alcohol. Take that away and watch me turn to dust. Never mind, I'll do it myself.

I rationalized that my world had become inconsequential, and it didn't matter. People would be better off without me than with the me they didn't want. I didn't see myself as alcoholic. I drank mostly beer. I only drank the hard stuff when beer wasn't available. It never occurred to me to not drink anything or to have a soft drink instead. I surrounded myself with people who drank worse than I did, so I could say, "See, I'm not that bad." I thought an alcoholic was synonymous with a skid row bum. I wasn't wearing tattered clothes, smelling like a wet camel, and begging for change. I wasn't carrying a brown paper sack with my half pint in it. I can't be an alcoholic.

When I attended meetings, I looked at the people in the room and thought, *I wouldn't even drink with these people*. I was angry, shut down, and resentful. I was despondent. I don't know how you can be defiant and despondent at the same time, but I managed. I kept everyone at arm's length, and I shared nothing and admitted nothing. I didn't want to deal with another issue. I struggled every day to not commit suicide because alcohol wasn't doing it fast enough.

I participated in more meetings, against my better judgment, and despite my defiance, I sensed and heard something. I did not want to relate to these people. But I was in a group of people who didn't judge, didn't reject differences, and who accepted even if they didn't understand or hadn't shared the same experience. I saw no raised eyebrows. They said welcome and come back. I thought I felt the pressure ease, and maybe I found a source of strength. After a month or so of attending the meetings, I had a life-altering experience that went deep, hit hard, and changed the course of my future.

* * *

Regina, Doris's mother, had been diagnosed with cancer, and the prognosis was not good. Doris's parents were living in Germany at the time, and it was winter. Cold, damp, and lonely was not the environment for a cancer patient. Doris and I invited Regina to come and live with us in warm, sunny, cozy Arizona.

I Always Wanted to Be Your Hero

Chet, Regina's husband, had requested a transfer back to Detroit, and it would be a few months before all the *i*'s could be dotted and the *t*'s crossed on that plan. So Regina came to live with us in the interim. When the position in Detroit was finalized, she would move to Michigan and get the care she needed by her husband's side. We did our best to make her feel comfortable and safe. It was always about being safe. When you're weak, fighting, lonely, or lost, it's not always about the fix; it's about being safe. I grew up in a predictable, safe environment. Predictable meant safe. I knew what came next, even if I didn't like it. I knew what to expect when I opened the door and went out. I felt safe and could handle any minor variances from the day's plan. Predictability had abandoned me, but I wanted to keep Regina safe.

What If Something Else Were to Go Wrong?

Regina arrived from Germany, shivering and thin as a rail. The cancer had taken its toll. She was four feet eleven and not more than seventy-five pounds soaking wet. What had not been scorched by cancer yet was her beautiful face crowned with long flaming red curly hair and her occasional smart quip and smile.

Regina grew weaker by the day. She kept falling and hurting herself especially at night when she needed a bathroom break. It became so bad that the falls and the injuries became routine. Doris and I decided that we needed to go on twenty-four-hour duty to ensure Regina didn't fall and hurt herself. The night shifts would be the most difficult. I worked outside the house, and Doris had the kids underfoot during the day. Our initial plan to cover the night shifts consisted of each of us rotating with each other, two hours on and two hours off.

In the mornings, I went off to work, and Doris managed the daytime routines of three kids and a mom in residence. We curbed the falls and the injuries, but we got tired and cranky at each other over any tiny perceived misstep.

This wasn't going to work. I was reminded of a lesson I should have learned in Nam. Just admit we were not skilled at this, or we couldn't handle this role.

* * *

I didn't learn that lesson because my memories, locked away, prevented me from doing so. I didn't remember until I visited the Vietnam War Memorial in Washington, DC, in 2012. Fear of unleashing the demons prevented me from going sooner. I placed my palm over the etchings of those that died and wondered why. Pride had won out, and it cost us dearly. We treated people who were not skilled and adept at certain tasks as failures—like I felt Dad had treated me. We had difficulty recognizing the truth.

We should engage in the things we like, those things we are competent at, and those that bring us joy. When we embrace them, we shine. Being the star of the play, not the star quarterback gave me joy. Banging our heads against a wall of darkness or failure benefits no one. If we continue doing that, someone who loves us needs to stand up and say no. If we could have said no to the pilot who was failing and who ultimately crashed the plane in Da Nang, imagine the lives and suffering we could have spared.

Doris and I were not trained caretakers. It would have been better to bring someone in or set Regina up in a facility that could take care of her. It wasn't that we didn't love her or want to keep her safe and comfortable; we just didn't know how. We didn't have the resources to provide what she needed.

* * *

One weekend night, I decided to stay on duty all evening and let Doris get some rest. I was always seeking solutions and thought I could handle this. I did not have to work the next day, and I could sleep in. We tucked Regina in, and Doris headed off for her two-hour nap, not aware that I intended to let her sleep. I packed some snacks, my beer, and the remote for the TV, and settled in the recliner in Regina's bedroom. I was going to be her knight in shining armor. For a drunk like me, though, the armor doesn't shine, and the knight couldn't not drink.

Sometime in the middle of the night, I fell asleep in the lounge chair. Meaning, I passed out. I was startled awake by a tugging on the pant leg of my jeans. I bolted up and looked down to see nothing but a bloody mess. Regina had risen and attempted to travel across the hall to the bathroom, but she didn't make it. She fell hitting her face on the corner of the dresser. Now that lovely face wasn't so lovely, and I was responsible. I washed her face and put her back in bed, feeling despondent and more strongly than ever that I was not the son-in-law she could have wanted.

Regina was tucked tightly under her covers. I stood over her, not knowing what to do. If I sat back in my chair, I might fall asleep again, and it was too early to wake Doris. So I lay on top of the covers fully dressed and held Regina through the night to ensure she didn't get up and fall again. I didn't trust myself to be there for someone I loved. I couldn't even manage the normal routine of waking and sleeping. Regina woke the next morning, called her husband in Germany, and left our house shortly after, and I never saw her again.

Is This What You Do to People You Love?

Despondent, alone, and lost, I ran from the house. To stay was to potentially hurt more people I loved. Now the awful reality of me was undeniable. I was a drunk, and I hurt those I loved. I left Doris, Debby, Julie, and Matt on their own. First, Doris's mother moved out, and then I did the same. What a terrible burden for Doris to bear. Life shouldn't have treated her that way. I shouldn't have treated her that way. But I had to do it.

I didn't know what was worse—the hurt I inflicted on others or the pain I felt. Maybe it didn't matter, pain is pain, and maybe a drink could make it go away. Even I was not fooled by that notion anymore. What to do, when alcohol turned on me and was no longer my friend, terrorized me. My solution, to drink, no longer offered the reprieve and no longer worked.

Time to Die

I ran. I was not sure if I was running to something or away from something. I was just running. To stand still and do nothing was no longer possible. I didn't have another solution

I ended up with Sebastian, the only place I felt safe. But the *safe* didn't last. No matter where I ran, I had to take myself along. The problems became the shadows that followed. Running didn't make them go away. Running didn't leave them behind. Adrift in a morass of sorrow with a history of hurting others and no solution, I felt cornered. I needed relief; I needed a way out. I decided I had to die, and all that remained was the when and how.

Decision Made; I'm Leaving

I lived from moment to moment, going through the days, putting one foot in front of the other as I contemplated a way out. I had been introduced to a recovery program, and I knew it had helped others, but I was different; it wouldn't work for me.

I went to more meetings with Sebastian and sat there with nothing behind me but loss, and I couldn't look back. I couldn't look at the present because if I met anyone's eyes, the pain I'd caused would be visible, and they might even see my secret. When I tried to look ahead to the future, I saw nothing. Nothing is the absence of everything, including hope. How could I visualize a future in a world that didn't have room for me? In a world with a narrow alley of acceptance and very rigid rules I couldn't follow. In a world I was not even sure I wanted to live in, never mind could live in? No way forward and no way back.

I thought I might as well quit drinking just to prove it wasn't a problem. I went for a few days, maybe a week, and convinced myself it wasn't a problem. "Much ado about nothing." It's time for a drink. I rationalized that it had nothing to do with the anxiety I felt or the jitters I experienced. Or that I thought about drinking 24-7. I had just finished cleaning a small two-bedroom apartment, and everyone knows the reward for cleaning was to have a drink.

I walked two blocks to the corner grocery store and bought one can of beer. See, I'm not an alcoholic. Alcoholics would buy at least a six-pack or a pint or more. Not me. I carried the single can in a brown paper bag back to the apartment and set it on the coffee table. A flashback about brown paper bags and people who used them caused me momentary pause. I ritualistically began drinking the can of beer. I picked it up, took a small sip, and put it down. I waited a few minutes to prove I had power over alcohol. It did not control me. I picked the can up and repeated the process. On the third *controlled* sip, Sebastian opened the door and entered. He was not supposed to be home for at least another hour. I had promised him I wouldn't drink. He walked behind the sofa and came around to sit by me. I quickly picked up the opened can of beer, hoping he hadn't seen it and tried to stuff it into my pants pocket. That didn't work.

I was overweight, the pants were old, and there was no excess *pocket* to accommodate the unfinished beer. I looked like I'd peed myself again.

The realization hit hard. I had no power over drinking. One beer proved it, and I didn't even get to finish it. I had justified my drinking believing everyone else drank like me or worse. Not true. I had surrounded myself only with people who drank like me or worse so I would look good. I frequently said, "So what? I'm not hurting anyone with my drinking." Now I hurt so much and had hurt so many people I couldn't lie. I added, *You don't deserve to live if this is what you do to the people you love,* to my rationale for suicide.

I went to a meeting that night, and out of desperation, I stood and said, "My name is Joe, and I'm an alcoholic."

* * *

I had been attending meetings for about a month and a half. The money odds in the meetings were that I was never going to admit to my problem. When I said I'm an alcoholic, the participants of the meeting broke out clapping and cheering. I got to the point of surrender out of desperation, not inspiration. I realized that I was addicted to alcohol. I was here because this was the last house on the block. There was nowhere for me to go. No way forward and no way back. Get help or get out.

I could not imagine living without alcohol. Feeling all the negative feelings all the time. Feeling unsafe at every turn. Feeling alone and unloved. Alcohol was my solution, not my problem. Take away my solution, and I would feel this way forever. I was not sure this was a solution, but I knew I could not drink again. If I did, I would hurt someone I loved again or myself. Myself seemed like the better alternative.

A New and Terrible Fear Surfaced: What If I Lived?

I said I was an alcoholic the day before I died. The day before I died by my own hand, and no one could say how many days I had left before I drank myself to death if I chose that route. That could have been my next tomorrow or worse, years more of darkness and pain.

The twelve-step program was created by people who knew how I, and others like me, felt. Alcohol did not solve my problems; it just masked them for another day before they sneaked back into my head and haunted me. If I practiced what I heard and what members of the program taught me, I could be free of pain and hurt. I could learn to love and have hope again. I could learn to love me as the people on this journey with me loved me. I did not fully believe this would work, but I only had one other option, and I hesitated to opt for it. I didn't have the courage to do it.

As I began recovery, the suicide solution took a back seat to discovery. Discovering a new way forward. I started the journey back from the edge. Step by small step, one day at a time, sometimes one minute at a time.

Through the process, I defined me, and in doing so, I took my power back. I learned who and what I was and to accept me as the person I had become. I also learned who I was *not*. I defined myself in real terms, not through images of media or TV. Not the images in someone else's head.

When I denied I was gay, and someone called me fag, I was devastated. When I defined myself as gay, and someone used that term, I was offended. Big difference between devastated and offended. There was no power in the label because I owned it, wore it, and lived in a real world.

I learned this Vietnam vet, son, father, ex-husband, brother, friend, and lover was enough. I was going to be okay. I just wanted to know, to my core, that I was enough. I just wanted to feel safe and know I would be okay getting up and going out the door. In Vietnam, the days and nights were not predictable. Life was not predictable. When I put my head on the pillow at the end of the day, I did not know if a rocket might hit close by or if I would wake to see the new day's sun.

I thought the antidote to unsafe was predictability, but that was not true. Life anywhere is unpredictable. In redefining me, I learned that I could survive whatever life presented. I was challenged often to rethink that premise, but the new bottom line always ended with *I know I can survive*. I had what I needed. I had my power back and a power greater than myself that I could turn to and be assured in times of doubt.

Over the years, when serious trauma struck, and I felt myself slipping back, I had to redefine myself again to live in whatever new reality was created. The new me rose from the ashes time and time again. I was taught I had everything I needed to be successful. The power of me came from within. I was looking outside myself for strength, wisdom, and courage. Look within and know it's there—feel it.

I learned how to engage in life, my life, as it presented itself. I lived day by day and dealt with what was in front of me. I planned for the future, but I did not plan the outcome. Fortunately, I didn't plan the outcome; things turned out better than my wildest dreams. The lesson in this practice was that, if engaged, I was closer to a potential solution to resolve those things I didn't like. One issue for me was, I had to define my body image as it was and admit maybe I was built for comfort and not speed.

I worked out, dieted, and changed that image. I couldn't do that sitting on the couch with a bag of chips. I engaged with how I defined myself and only changed those things that dissatisfied me. I engaged. If it wasn't image, maybe the solution was to get more education. I returned to school and got a master's degree. Maybe the solution was to get a different job. I polished up the résumé, became a management consultant, worked in human resources, and made a contribution. Maybe the solution was to create a circle of friends that accepted me and loved me unconditionally. I am now rich with friends, some for more than forty years.

Being totally isolated and alone, I could not change anything. There were no people to advise, guide, and show me the way. No one to share their experience, strength, and hope. Once I engaged, I could see the success and failures of others and learn from them. I could be there for them as well.

I got connected—connected with me, with others, and with a purpose in life. My life grew. It wasn't so small anymore. Bit by bit, new people, new travels, new experiences, and new memories were created. Those experiences were shared with laughter and tears. Some of those new experiences were not positive, but they were mine. I created a history. A history I could look at with pride, even when there were failures and missteps. Having a history is a great and powerful gift. It's unique, it's mine and mine alone, it's added to day by day, and it can be shared with others to help show them the way home.

It was simple but not easy.

Chapter Fourteen

I DIDN'T DO IT

Many moments and seconds of my life had been painful. Moments of hurt seemed as if they would go on forever. Seconds of scorn cut to the marrow of my existence. I thought, *No accumulation of time would make you love me.* No deeds were great or good enough for me to earn your respect. There were no more ribbons or rewards for going on.

I Didn't Want to Be Here. Taking My Life Wasn't Fearful. Being Here Was

Thinking of no tomorrows didn't generate anxiety and sadness. Wondering what would come next did. What form of hurt lurked around the next corner? Wrestling with whether I could endure the next barrage of hate and contempt exhausted me. Constantly worrying, "would I be okay?" was a heavy burden.

Suicide had not been a threat to me; it was a viable option. It was a simple step to freedom from those oppressing moments and seconds. It was a solution. It was the appropriate exit for the coward, the "baby killer," and the vet no one saw or heard. It was the answer to the echoing mantra: and you never will be.

But I Didn't Do It

If I did, I would have killed the wrong person.

I would not have killed the person Dad wanted me to be because that person never existed.

I would not have offed the fat little kid mocked and humiliated because I wasn't fat.

I would not have ended the life of the little gay boy no one could accept.

I would not have killed the coward, the failure, and the unwanted lost child.

I would have killed the wrong person.

I would have killed the brave little boy who put his coat on and went for help. I would have ended the life of the loving father, husband, brother, and friend. I would have taken out the Vietnam vet who fought for freedom, the young man who made good decisions, and the somewhat handsome guy who is funny and often loved by friends, coworkers, and neighbors.

I would have killed the wrong person.

I was not the mocking phrases of my past. I was not lost or forgotten. My history was not a predictor of my future. My history is a foundation to build on and to recognize the strength and courage it took to make that history and survive it.

I let my brain do my thinking, and my emotions rule my actions. I should have thought more with my emotions and let my brain decide my actions. Emotions are an important part of me because I'm human, but they don't rule me. A balance of thought and emotions—an awareness of my humanity, my vulnerability, and my strengths—and the courage to rebuild me from the ground up was my way forward.

I embraced the program of recovery, which was a simple design for living. All I had was a design for dying. What I needed was a design to go on and create a future that didn't look dark and a present that wasn't full of conflict and pain. I now knew what waited for me if I drank again. I wouldn't get to start over. I would pick up right where I left off, and if I drank again, I honestly believe that would be the next day before I died.

I became attached to recovery fast and furious because that community accepted me as I was. I got to define myself and engage in a life I could learn to love and respect. Like Grandma Josephine, if they didn't know, it didn't matter. If they did, *live and let live.* I could talk to people in the program, and they listened. It was a band of men and women without that judgmental look in their eyes when I shared my secrets. They were like the men in Vietnam that held me and said, "We're going to make it through the night."

Not the Day Before the End—Just a Beginning, Just a Chance

I realized that I had come by my addiction honestly. I believe alcoholism is a disease. The American Medical Association supports that theory. I don't use that knowledge to abdicate responsibility for my problem. Instead, I see an analogy between my disease and any other. Diabetes is just one example. Yes, that's a disease no one wants and a disease that may have been acquired genetically. But it's not okay for anyone to keep passing out from a sugar imbalance in their system.

I was faced with this exact situation at work. A man with diabetes kept forgetting or refusing to take his insulin. He kept passing out on the factory floor. This was dangerous to himself and a potential danger to others. I told him in a coaching session, "We will accommodate and support you in any way possible, but you and only you are responsible for the solution to your disease. Take your insulin."

For me, don't drink. The consequences for either of us to refuse to manage our diseases was possible termination. (Pun intended.)

PART THREE

Because I Lived

Temporary problems do not call for permanent solutions.

Chapter Fifteen

HEALING

The problem was in the perceptions I had created about myself and the world in which I lived. I believed I wasn't good enough, and that if people knew that, I wouldn't be accepted or loved. I thought the world I lived in was one that would never make room for me to live in it peacefully. These ideas led me to believe I wasn't safe in this skin, as this person living in this world.

My views of me and my world were intricately wrapped around my ego. Alcoholics are the only people I know who are egomaniacs with an inferiority complex. I went to a psychiatrist, and after examining me, he said, "I know why you have an inferiority complex." I said, "Oh, why?" And he said, "Because you're inferior." Just kidding.

It really wasn't about me. When Dad yelled at me because I went next door for help, it wasn't because I was stupid, cowardly, or weak. When I fell out of the car, I was obeying what I thought Mom said. When Mom got hurt in the car crash, it wasn't that I caused it. North Korea shooting down our plane had nothing to do with me or my performance. I felt like I might as well have been the one that fired the kill shot. Regina got hurt because she was weak and ill. It wasn't my fault; it wasn't all about me. I thought ego was me thinking I was all that and a bag of chips, but it was not. Ego was me thinking all that happens is because of me or about me. The world has a mind of its own, but most people in this world react based on their own perceptions and emotions.

Dad got angry because he was embarrassed. I didn't know at seven that you shouldn't open the door of a moving vehicle. I wasn't driving either vehicle when Mom was injured, and she wanted to get out of the house more than I did. I warned that crew not to fly too close to North Korea, but they did anyway. And I didn't fire any of those kill shots, but I chose to be the one who was wounded.

I thought if anyone had my life, they'd drink too. Life was out to get me. The truth is, life is life. Life goes on whether we like it or not. We don't get to control life. I had to learn to alter my reactions to life. I didn't know because I was too young or too inexperienced to ask if there was another possible interpretation to life's events other than I'm a loser. Some people may find it easy to just blame others, but responsibility and blame are not synonymous. I am responsible for me, my actions and reactions only. How the world and my circle of friends respond to me is none of my business. I get to say, "See me." I get to carve out and cultivate a safe place for me, and I get to choose my friends.

I also had to learn humility. Humility, as I define it, is me being all I can be, not shrinking from the skill set that I have or pretending to have skills I don't. Accepting my limitations as well, not taking responsibility for things that are out of my control, not choosing to take the blame for other's shortcomings. It might have sounded like, *Yes, Dad, I did go next door because you left us alone, and we were afraid. And yes, Dad, I thought that was a good and brave thing to do.* Sorry you disagree.

But it's also accepting when I am at fault and atoning for any misdoings. Humility is being the best me I can be and using the gifts I've been given to the best of my abilities.

I'm not a concert pianist, and that's okay although I'd like to entertain the world with beautiful music. I'm not a coward, and yet I fear, and that's okay. I make some good decisions and some dreadful decisions. I love and lose. I laugh and cry, and sometimes I fail because I'm human. Most of all, I'm me, and today I'm proud of the me I've become.

Joseph Campbell said, "Each of us has a meaning, and we bring that meaning to life." There is no blueprint for life, but there is meaning to it, and the mystery is we don't always know what that meaning is because it's not about us. The lessons we experience may not be for us or about us. We may just be instruments to help others grow and blossom. The true tragedy would be to take a life and eliminate what was meant to be.

Chapter Sixteen

NEED TO KNOW

They had to know; I had to tell them. They would want to know, wouldn't they? This was me starting over. I couldn't keep secrets. I couldn't hide, and I was not going forward with someone else's version of my life. It was mine, and I was responsible—good or bad, accepted or rejected. I couldn't distinguish between bravery and desperation, but in the end, it didn't matter. Desperation made me say I'm an alcoholic and begin the journey of recovery. Bravery and courage reinstilled by the members of my program allowed me to stand up and say this is my truth, this is who I am, and let's begin the journey of discovery together.

On a hot Arizona summer day with the temperatures well above one hundred degrees, I summoned Mom and Dad to the kitchen table in their home to tell them. I was dressed in shorts only, no shirt, no socks, no shoes, and as I faced off against the solemn expressions on the faces of my parents, I began shivering. I did not frequently summon my parents. It was more like they summoned me. But I said I needed to have an important discussion, and they obliged. Because I felt so cold, I raced back to the bedroom I was staying in and put on a shirt. I came back to the table babbled on about nothing, and the shivering got worse. My teeth were chattering, my knees were knocking, and

226

I couldn't utter a word. I raced to the bedroom again, and this time, I put on a pair of jeans. Back to the table but still freezing even though you could fry eggs on the sidewalks of Mesa.

Stuttering and stammering, I stalled by talking about my physical condition, wondering why I felt so cold. Was I coming down with something? Dad finally said, "Stop stalling. Out with it now." The ever so infamous *now*. Maybe it was just this one last time that I had to hear *now*. Maybe that word had always been for me to be in the now as me and not hiding. I blurted out, "I'm gay."

Dad instantaneously responded, and I mean instantaneously with, "You know I could have gone my whole life without hearing this." Silence. Then he said, "It's okay if it's the neighbor's kid. It's not okay if it's my kid." Hmm, my perception of "they needed" to know or they "would want" to know might need recalculating. I had not taken a breath in the last sixty seconds, and this response justified the shivering.

Mom didn't say a word. She slowly and softly rose from the table and moved to an adjoining family room where she began dusting. I was in a tomb of silence, only broken by the soft sound of a thick cloth brushing over a coffee table and end tables and the occasional *pssst* from the can of Pledge as Mom shined and reshined dust-free furniture.

I looked at Dad and finally said, "I'm worried about her." He said to just let her be. "She processes everything internally, and when she's ready to talk about it, she will. I, on the other hand, process everything out loud." No kidding. His final volley that morning was, "You're our son, and we'll try to deal with this."

We'll try to deal with this? I would have done anything not to be gay. I tried everything to deal with it from priests to therapists, and nothing changed. In my former reality, being gay was not okay. I understand why some people take their life when they get exhausted trying to maintain a facade about who they are and refusing to act on the love they so strongly feel. I listened to those who said it's a choice, and I listened to those who said if you accept God, you won't feel that way, and all I got was pain. I realized those who thought differently have never lived with that kind of pain. It was just another venue for judgment and rejection.

I came to my parents and said I'm gay not because they needed to know. What I had to say wasn't as important as that I had to say it. I came to them and revealed myself to move on in recovery. I came out and continued the process of getting sober. There wasn't another option; I would have taken it if there was.

Let's Hope This Works

During that visit, not another word was said about my secret that would eventually become the white elephant of the homogenous New England, Irish Catholic family. And we weren't done until I told them I was also an alcoholic. Is the brass ring within reach?

Dad later said he would assume the daunting task of telling the nine brothers and sisters about this anomaly called Joe. I argued that it was my responsibility, and after a few rounds, I knew I would lose; I conceded. I conceded right after Dad shared his logic with me about why he should be the one to tell everyone. He said, "I don't want a faction for Joe and a faction against Joe. If they see your mom and I struggling with this, then they, too, may try to find a way to deal with it."

In his travels over the next few months, Dad told all my siblings that I was of the gay persuasion. Some of the scenes were much like the frigid kitchen table tableau in Mesa. Dad would sit with a sib or two, stutter and stammer, and have difficulty blurting out the news. On one such occasion, one of my brothers said, "Thank God, it's just that he's gay. You were making such a production of this. I thought you were going to tell us Joey was dying of cancer." Would it really have been easier to say I had cancer than to say I was gay? Well, it was the dark ages of the seventies and eighties.

Mom did not speak to me on this subject for nine months. Our relationship was extremely functional. Hello, goodbye, when will you be visiting next? Nine months almost to the day, as if reliving my birth, I got a letter from Mom. The letter said, "You are my son, and I love you. But do not talk about this issue, and do not joke about your lifestyle." Mom went on to say, "If you come to town and you are alone, you can stay at our house. If you come to town and you are with someone, get a hotel room."

My brothers tried to put a little levity into the situation by cracking jokes. The most notable being when we were enjoying a barbecue on top of South Mountain during our Phoenix family reunion. Someone snapped a picture of older brother Billy, me in a cowboy hat and leather jacket, and our younger, fitter brother Paul. The caption under the photo became "The Lawyer, the Jock, and the Fruit." Now I don't practice law, and I'm not a thrower, so you can guess which one was me.

We developed coded communications around the gay issue. When I wanted to visit, I would call Mom and say I'm coming to town on such and such a date and could I stay with you, she would instantly know I was coming alone. When I would call and say could you please make me reservations at a nearby hotel, she would know I was not coming alone. This worked, and we never mentioned gay or anything about me that was substantive or important. It was enough for me to recognize they did not want to know, they did not have to know, and they would have preferred to go to their graves not having to deal with this. I told them because it was important to me, and I wanted them to know so I could live.

I called what came next the process of accepting, understanding, and loving. This was going to be a long process, a very long process, not an event. Just because I said it doesn't mean they got it. I had to allow them to go through their own process of acceptance and get to a comfortable, loving place for themselves, as I had done for me. Sometimes that takes years. I couldn't stay out of that process, of course. During this getting-to-know-you phase, I was asked to speak at a conference in San Diego sponsored jointly by the Gay Academic Union of a local college and the support and advocacy group Parents and Friends of Lesbians and Gays. The chairwoman identified the topic as the coming out process. She asked me to share who I came out to, how it went, and what was going on now. If that wasn't chilling enough, she went on to say, "Oh, it would be great if you'd invite the people, especially parents, you came out to so they can share their experience and thoughts as well."

I really wanted to invite Mom and Dad, but given the frigid reception I got, I wasn't sure that was the most appropriate action. I thought about this so much that I got those chills again. I finally got to the place where I knew I wanted this for me, and I could accept any answer. It was not going to be easy for them. If they said yes, it was a gift to me. If they said no, it was an indication we still had much work to do. So I made the phone call. I relayed the request. "Would you come to California, sit in front of a large audience, and share your experience, thoughts, and feelings with an auditorium full of strangers about the day your son told you he was gay?"

Return to the Tomb of Silence.

After a moment or two, Dad said, "We'll think about it and get back to you." The click and buzz of the dead line was ominous.

A few days later, I got a call, and Dad said, "We'll be there." He delivered this simple, straight-to-the-point statement with no further discussions.

We arrived at the college on the day of the workshop and were directed to the stage where we would be seated facing that crowd of strangers. The contingent of speakers included a lesbian couple seated on the left as you faced the stage, the moderator in the middle, and me and my partner on the right of the moderator. All of us had two family members or friends we brought with us to share. The moderator started on the left with the lesbian couple, and one by one, we shared our experiences. Six people in all shared, and I don't remember a word. I was one breath away from shock and being comatose from worrying about what my team was going to do and say. The progression of sharing continued through my partner and his guests. Then it came down to us.

We were the last family to share. Dad first, me next, and Mom on the far right-hand side. As time wore on, she gradually fell apart. Quietly, she clutched a handkerchief that started out neatly ironed and folded and now looked like a raisin. Dad shared, and he said exactly what he said to me that day I came out to them. "I could have gone my entire life without hearing this. It's okay if it's the neighbor's kid. It's not okay if it's my kid."

Mom's sobs increased in volume as Dad shared. Dad goes on for a while about telling the rest of the family, and he spoke in a sound and stoic manner. I shared, and I don't remember what I said. Now all eyes were on Mom. She was visibly distraught,

crying and wringing her hands around the mutilated and shred-
ded raisin, I mean hankie. Her head hung down almost to her
lap, and she was silent. The auditorium followed suit and went
silent. For a brief second, I was reliving the silence of Vietnam
just before the rockets hit. You could have heard a pin drop.
After what seemed like an eternity, Mom raised her head looked
into the eyes of the audience and, with a forceful burst of anger,
said, "Well, I'm here, aren't I?"

Not another word was spoken. After a few moments of
stunned silence, the audience, as one, rose to their feet and gave
Mom a standing ovation. Testimony to the courage and love
it took just to show up. We don't have to be eloquent; we just
need show up for the ones we love. We still had much work
to do, but the amazing revelation that day was that we had a
chance. We might just make it through this struggle.

* * *

Some months later, I called Mom and said, "I'm coming to
town, would you be kind enough to make a reservation for me at
a hotel?" Code alert: I'm not coming alone. I also tell Mom that
finances were a bit tight, so please find modest accommodations
for us that won't break the bank. A few days later, Mom called
back and said, "I think you'll love the place I've found for you."

I said, "Oh, good. Where?"

She said, "Stay here with us."

Welcome Home

We made it. Another breakthrough, another milestone,
and I felt astounded and elated. We arrived at my parent's
home, and Mom says, "You can have Susie's room." The only

room, other than the master, that had one bed. That was way above and beyond the call of duty, and I didn't dare say a word.

My partner and I slept together the first night. The bed was only a double bed. He was over six feet tall, and I move around in my sleep like I'm running an obstacle course. It was pure hell. We didn't sleep a wink. The next day, I said, "Mom, I appreciate you giving us Susie's room, but the bed is too small. Could we move to the boy's room?" That room had twin beds. We pushed the beds together and slept soundly in the home of people who had never entertained the idea of gay, never mind the thought that their son might be gay. Give them time, allow the process, and miracles can happen.

Decades later, my two youngest brothers came out as gay. Yes, I believe it's genetic. Ellen DeGeneres once cracked a joke about gays earning a toaster for converting straights to gay. I didn't earn a toaster. These two brothers had had a pact for years. The terms of the pact were, if one of them came out to Mom and Dad, they were to drag the other out of the closet, kicking and screaming at the same time. I might have done some trailblazing for them, but they still had severe reservations about coming out. What added to that angst was Dad's original statement to me about going his whole life without needing to hear about it and, of course, Mom's pain. The bravest soul of the two was the youngest son. David had been in a committed relationship with a man named Glenn for years. David sat down with Mom and Dad and said, "I'm gay, and oh, by the way, so is Charlie," like he was buying tickets to the US Open. Oh yeah, Charlie's going too!

Dad immediately called me and asked if I knew about Charlie and David. I said I did, not having to ask what it was that I was supposed to know. I knew and kept silent waiting for the day I'd have company on this deserted island and not be adrift with my uniqueness. Dad angrily said, "Three out of

233

seven sons. That's more than 10 percent." The popular belief at that time was 10 percent of the population was gay, and Dad was a bit chagrined his family population topped those rates.

The predominant emotion when I was coming out to my parents and sibs was fear. What if they rejected and abandoned me? What if I'm not the son or the brother they wanted? Pain, overwhelming pain, was what I experienced when I had to tell my wife and children that I was not the husband or the father they wanted.

In 1977, I asked Doris for a divorce. Initially, I did not tell her the reason was because I was gay. I probably just said I'm not happy or irreconcilable differences or some other vague half truth. That avoidance wasn't out of meanness or malice. It was because I hadn't fully reconciled me with myself, and I didn't want to hurt her more.

Later, as I saw the pain, hurt, and blame she was shouldering, coupled with my learning to speak my truth, I told her. I held her and said, "I'm sorry for all the pain I've caused you, and maybe someday, you can come to understand that I had to do this." The divorce became final ten years almost to the day after our wedding.

I decided the children needed to be told. We were months away from a Cape Cod family reunion. Since all my brothers and sisters knew the truth, I didn't want my children to hear it from a secondary source. That secondary source could be gossip, an offhanded comment, genuine curiosity, or just a simple question from someone who cared. I discussed this with Doris, and she decided to tell the children, at least the older two, herself, and she did. It was a similar situation to my Dad telling my brothers and sisters. The girls thought the news was that I had cancer or some other terminal illness. The girls told me later that Doris sat them on the couch and, after much hemming and hawing and talking around this difficult topic, told them their father was gay. It was dramatic, and I'm not sure they completely understood. Doris opted to not tell Matthew as she thought he was too young.

One weekend when I had the children at my parent's home, I took Matt aside and told him. I didn't want any surprises at the reunion for anyone. He was too young, and he had no reaction. What became the brick from the blindside was that daughter number two, Julie, reacted with the rage of a caged bull.

Julie felt I had blundered big-time, and she let me know it in no uncertain terms. She was screaming at me at the top of her lungs. Mom was getting very upset and concerned by the tirade. I guess she wanted Julie to just go quietly dust the family room. It was disruptive, so I took Julie into a bathroom at the back of the house and hopefully out of earshot or, at least, where the decibels of the din was reduced. We got behind closed doors, and I just let her vent. She went on for what seemed like forever. It wasn't. It just went on until her anger exhausted her. When silence came, I just held her and said, "Wouldn't it be easier if you just hated me? I know you don't, and I love you, too." We cried.

There is no blueprint, no stencil, or structure to guide you in matters like these. You must trust that love is strong enough to overcome. Hopefully, love will win in the moment, and the pain will not be protracted. When that's not the case, know that love eventually does win. My son, as he grew up, had great difficulty accepting the truth of me. He had difficulty separating the truth of me from the truth of him and the truth of his mother.

After a long and tenuous relationship, Matt called me. He was in his late teens. He advised me that he and his girlfriend were headed to Disneyland and wanted to stop by and say hello. I was very excited to be included in his life. Plans for a very nice dinner began, which means I made reservations at an upscale

Italian restaurant in North County. My cooking skills might have threatened the well-being of all involved and ruined the night. I anxiously awaited their arrival. The day finally came, and we sat down; Matt sat in front of me, and his girlfriend beside me in a nice candlelit environment. The introductions and small talk ended in about three minutes, and Matt fired his first salvo of rockets by saying, "I'm really having difficulty with this fag thing."

After a long, stunned, pregnant pause, I said, "It's okay that you're having trouble with this. I had trouble with it myself. Please know that it's a process, not an event. It will take time. I'm very happy that you are willing to talk with me and attempt to understand." I then went on to say, "As you struggle with this process, don't ever, ever use the term fag again. Let me give you some alternative words you can use." I came to realize using that descriptor may not have been malicious or deliberate. That was the only term he knew to describe me. No one, including me, had taken the time to discuss the acceptable from the unacceptable.

I tossed a few alternate descriptors on the table, like homosexual, gay, and alternative lifestyle. I did the best I could on the spur of the tense moment, realizing that just because I made a grand announcement didn't mean it got a grand reception. I was still new at this too. Often, many people struggle to understand differences, especially when it's new and awkward for them.

Matt worked hard that night and continues to work to understand, to accept, and to include me in his life to the best of his ability. He's doing great. One premise of his decision to work through this and find some peace with the fact that his father was gay was his children. He felt strongly that he didn't want them to miss the opportunity of knowing their grandfather. Another milestone, another gift.

That night, we discussed the Catholic views on homosexuality. That didn't take long; all gays were going to hell. We discussed the Catholic views on divorce, and that didn't take long either. Divorce was also wrong. We discussed the genetic or hereditary, nature versus nurture aspect of homosexuality and came to no conclusion. The best I could offer was that I would have done anything to not be gay. I went to church, to counseling, to hell and back, to not be gay. I eventually accepted it because there was no other alternative. I had to live the life I had and not the one I thought others wanted me to live. In acceptance, I found the ability to appreciate and be proud of me. In the authentic me, I find strength and courage, not weakness and loss.

Chapter Seventeen

SILENCE'S END

The silence related to war and death ended in 2012. Dinner at a sushi restaurant with my granddaughter, Jessica created the opportunity. The sushi restaurant was painted in dark shades of red and black. A large gray mural of a fish adorned one wall. It might have been a throwback to Vietnam, only better decorated and more modern. Jessica beat me to the table and sat with her back to the wall and a view of the door. That would have forced me to sit facing the ugly fish and have my back to the door. I said, "No, no, honey. GPJ [Grampa Joe] sits there." The grandchildren had begun calling me GPJ. It sounded better than Grampa, which made me feel old. I endorsed the new moniker, and the nickname was soon adopted by all. I liked it. Jessica focused on the seating arrangement said, "Why do you need to sit here, so you can see everyone coming and going and be Mr. Social?"

"No," I said. "So I can see the grenade when it's thrown through the door."

The look on Jessica's face can only be described as a mixture of shock and awe. Silently, I realized those words had never been spoken out loud before. For over forty years, I sat with my back to a wall as a requirement but never told anyone why.

The doors to the past burst opened. These doors did not gently and gradually open; they just burst like someone opened a bottle of champagne, and the bubbly was arching toward the ceiling. After the initial awkward silence created by us treading in unknown territory. Jessica said, "GPJ, you never talk about Vietnam. I'd like to hear your stories."

And the Healing Began

That night, I talked about the funny stories and the heroics of others. I talked about the people and the places her grandmother and I lived, and I talked about life. In this sharing, I remembered that life was going on and moving forward while I was in a freeze-frame of brown. We talked about the birth of her mother Debby, Aunt Julie, and Uncle Matt; we talked about new friends that her grandmother Doris and I made and new alliances that were forged with the people of Japan and Vietnam. I began to recall the good and the beauty of living in magnificently different cultures.

The realization that beautiful and atrocious happenings can occur at the same time pushed its way to the surface. Why did the pain, not the good, occupy most of my mind? I only saw the sad, not the joy. Pain doesn't eliminate good. Sad doesn't eliminate happiness. They just sit parallel to each other, waiting for us to look and to see beyond our pain and sadness. The shocking lesson was that all emotions are temporary. Unfortunately, even the good ones. Sadness, grief, and loss seemed to overwhelm me, and I thought those feelings would go on forever. Pain is sometimes a precursor or pathway to the action necessary to change directions toward good. If only I could have seen both and known that I'd make it through the night.

I had waited forty-plus years to begin the healing on that level. The walls of my illusions and delusions no longer stand as a barrier to the real me.

I Am No Longer Lost and Defenseless

I no longer use alcohol as the mortar for a wall that keeps me away from people. When this titanic shift occurred, when I chose to face reality and no longer live in silence, I found the freedom we all fought for.

I had lost the ability to go back and pick up the pieces of my life, and I couldn't reach for the bootstraps to pull myself up because they were not my boots. Michael Ball wrote and sang a song that tells of living someone else's dream, feeling someone else's pain. That was me before. Now I knew I could be an authentic me.

We get to live our own dreams and, unfortunately, feel pain. But if I own it, I can cope and find peace. The new foundation I got with my recovery, and the lesson of seeing the beauty beyond the pain, were severely tested after forty years of sobriety.

* * *

Early on in my journey of sobriety, I grieved about leaving my children. One by one, I sat them down and made amends for leaving them. I said, "I'm so sorry I left you. Can you forgive me?" My oldest daughter, Debby, said, "Dad, you never left me. You've always been there for me."

Many Years Later, She Left Me

Debby, drank as I drank. That apple didn't fall far from the tree. She was extroverted, excited about life, and lived on the edge for years. She was married five times to four different men and could not find love or acceptance even though it was staring her in the face. She didn't know she was pretty, smart, and funny. She did not know how much we appreciated her. The drinking eventually robbed her of her health, her enjoyment of life, and her family.

Hello, Aunt Irene

On one of my visits, we shopped at Fashion Square in Scottsdale, Arizona. Breakfast at *Coco's* was always the first stop. While eating, I asked, "Do you know I love you? I want to make sure, no matter what, that you know I love you." She would always say, "Yeah, yeah, I know." On one occasion before shopping, I said, "Breakfast first." She said, "Oh, what another *Coco's* moment." She still grew up thinking she was not the daughter her father wanted.

She began exaggerating stories, living from crisis to crisis, and creating problems for herself and others. She would not listen, did not want the solutions I or her mother offered. She thought *we* were the crazy ones. I visited Scottsdale Christmas of 2017, my usual Christmas holiday. I wanted to visit family and have GPJ brunch. GPJ brunch was Grampa Joe taking all his granddaughters out for breakfast on December 24 and then shopping at the mall to get the girls something for Christmas. Yes, another *Coco's* moment. My planned visit that year with Debby never happened. She left town so I wouldn't see the devastating physically deterioration caused by her drinking. At breakfast with her daughters, I said, "You know your mother could die from this disease." Little did I know.

On a Saturday in February, Doris called and said Debby had fallen and injured herself and was in a Scottsdale hospital. I was living in Palm Springs at the time. I told Doris I would throw a few things in the car and be there quickly. She said, "No need to rush." Weak from health issues, Debby had fallen down a flight of stairs and was in a coma—less than two months from my warning to her children. For all intents and purposes, she was dead by the time she hit the bottom of the stairs. She ruptured her brain stem. Radical surgery was authorized by her husband and mother. The surgeons tried to save her by removing half of her skull to ease the pressure and removed a blood clot from the brain stem. When she came out of surgery, they told us the best we could hope for was that she would live in a vegetative state for the rest of her days.

My Daughter Was Gone

I looked at the shell of her and sat by the bedside with her mother for more than two days. The decision was made to take her off life support the following Tuesday. The pain of making that decision is not describable and was only surpassed by the actual event itself.

We stood around her bed as the end of life process began. It was a horror. She moved and twitched, and I silently called it signs of life. Hope sparked. She made gasping sounds as if trying to breathe. I found myself trying to breathe for her. Deep, long breaths that I was sure would reach her. Then she stopped breathing, and I did too. I didn't know how many seconds it was before I took the next breath, and I didn't care. I wondered why I continued to draw breath and why my heart rhythmically beat as it always had. The thought of going into the grave with her crossed my mind.

Grief, for me, is a different kind of pain. It comes in unpredictable waves. One moment I'm fine, and the next I'm lost in a ground swell of sorrow and being pulled under. Something will remind me of her—some sound, some word, a picture or a memory, and I feel the loss the same as I did on day 1. I can't say it ends because I don't know if it does. I can say I see the beauty of her as I feel the loss, and I know she is free from her demons. She is at peace and, unfortunately, did not live to know you can have peace in this life as well. I had to redefine myself as a man living with grief. I had to find times of laughter and love to balance the loss. I had to realize she was the one that died, not me.

In her book *Still Life*, Louise Penny refers to Brother Albert's theory on life: "Life is loss." Brother Albert refers to loss of parents, loss of loves, loss of jobs and security, and most importantly, loss of control. I can add loss of innocence, loss of defenses from the war, and loss of a daughter.

"We have to find a higher meaning in our lives other than those things and people. Otherwise, we'll lose ourselves. Life is loss, but out of that comes freedom. If we can accept that nothing is permanent and change is inevitable, if we can adapt, then we are going to be happier people. Change and loss may be the catalyst to go deep inside and find ourselves." As part of my healing, I did go deep inside and if I had not, I may have lost myself again with this tragedy. Brother Albert's book may be fictional, but life isn't.

I thought of a time she made me laugh, made me mad, and almost got me arrested as a terrorist. This occurred as we flew to West Virginia for my brother's funeral. He died of alcoholism a year and a half before Debby. He was found dead on his kitchen floor. Debby met me in Charleston and flew the last leg of the journey with me.

She was outrageous and had me laughing in this time of grief. I wish she was here to make me laugh now. When I think of that trip, I do laugh, so maybe she is doing just that.

On that trip, I was seated in the front row of a regional jet; the engines were revving, but no movement occurred. The plane had been delayed, waiting for something or someone. There was no mechanical or weather issue. Everyone was impatient and anxious as we waited. You could hear muttering and inappropriate comments passed from one passenger to another about the delay, the airline, and just about everything else. At the very last possible minute, my daughter came rushing up the ramp in a flurry of activity, noise and flowing silk. I thought it was Auntie Mame from the 1958 movie. But no, it was Debby. She sat in the seat next to me. Somehow she engineered a seat change, and we were side by side. Debby and her husband had just returned from Dubai, and as Debby threw herself into the assigned seat, she raised her leg and said, "How do you like my terrorist sandals?"

The look from the flight attendant could have chilled a summer day in Miami. I said, "Be quiet. Don't say that so loud, or we'll be arrested." The sandals had metal coins attached to a leather strap that wrapped around her ankles and up her calf. And she referred to them as terrorist sandals on two more occasions.

When I finally got her off the sandals topic, she began talking about her gay friends in Miami who were separated due to issues related to sex. Of course, she had to describe all the issues and did so in a detailed, graphic, and loud manner. I think the flight attendant was from the Bible Belt and did not appreciate the content of our conversation. She nicely leaned over and asked if we could keep it down a bit, but Debby's volume indicator left much to be desired. The second request from the flight attendant was just short of "Shut up." I was sure she had radioed ahead, and we were going to be arrested upon landing.

The jet landed at our destination, the door opened, and two agents of the airline blocked the exit. I heard one of them say they are trying to locate a Mr. Joseph Whitaker. We were right in the front; I wasn't eavesdropping. Now I knew for certain I was going to be arrested for entertaining a lady in terrorist sandals with a foul mouth. The stewardess, who was not the least bit happy with us, turned and pointed to me. Her arm was held high, chin level, her finger arched down with distain, and I couldn't hide. I got up from my seat and headed toward the agents who said, "Mr. Whitaker, could you wait over here, please?" Debby sauntered past us in her terrorist sandals, smiling and waving at me with her purse slung across her shoulder. I suppose that was a matching terrorist bag as well. She didn't even wait to see if I was being arrested.

After everyone deplaned, the agent who sequestered me said, "Sorry for the delay, sir, but your brother, who arrived on an earlier plane, lost his luggage, and we have it on this plane. Please be sure to pick it up for him at baggage claim."

I breathed a sigh of relief and raced down the ramp laughing and happy to be a free man. One emotion does not have to be all consuming. I could feel and share more. Pain shared is halved; joy shared is doubled. Share the pain until it's so small it's fleeting. Share the joy until your heart feels like it's going to burst.

We retold that story at least ten times, and each time the level of drama increased tenfold, the details got embellished, and I was all but put in handcuffs.

I'm smiling now through my tears, remembering this story. It made me even more determined not to drink nor to join her on her journey to the beyond. I chose to live.

That's hope.

Chapter Eighteen

RESENTMENTS

I may hold the record for carrying the longest resentment. It was going on forty years, carrying that gunnysack of anger on my back and packing bad karma. The awareness began as servicemen and women began returning from the Iraq and Afghanistan wars. I started noticing strange and odd things.

The first was when I boarded a plane for Chicago. The pilot came back and addressed a man in uniform, saying, "I have a seat open in first class. Please come forward. It's your seat. Thank you for your service." Well, hell, no one ever offered me a seat anywhere, never mind in first class. I started a slow gentle boil.

Next time, I was in a restaurant seated at a table for one and eating. Nearby was a soldier in uniform also eating at a table for one. A businessman in a suit and tie walked over, picked up the soldier's check and said, "I got this. Thank you for your service." I hold up my check, but he doesn't seem to notice, and I'm stuck paying my own bill. I would like to have been treated that way. No matter what branch, no matter what theater of conflict, just say "Thank you for your service." And while we're at it, let's thank the spouses of servicemen and woman as well. They also suffer in support of the fight for freedom.

One beautiful evening in San Diego, my friend Greg and I headed to check out a new dessert place in North Park. We entered a warm and aromatic environment that reminded me of the kitchen in Pennsylvania. One of the owner's greeting was equally as warm—his name was Lackland. He began telling us the story of the pastry shop. It was opened by five medics from Iraq, who were often confronted by wounded and frightened men and women on the field of battle who would ask, "Am I going home, or am I going to God?" And the medic's answer was, *"Either way, you are heaven sent."*

Heaven Sent, as the shop was named, took on meaning for me as well.

In the course of the discussion, I casually mentioned I served in Vietnam. It was a brief two-second sound bite, nothing of significance. Greg and I got our sweets, devoured them, and were headed out the door when Lackland said, "Hey, Joe, you got a sec?" I turned around, and he was holding a box of truffles tied with a red bow that he handed to me, saying, "Thank you for your service."

I wish I could express how much that meant, even forty years later. It was important, and it wasn't just a platitude. As he handed me the box of goodies, he said, "Man, what you guys did in Nam is still helping us today. Some of the lessons learned helped save lives in these current conflicts. You guys had it rough, so thank you."

I cried then, and I cry every time I think about it, and that's often.

The truffles stayed in my fridge way past their shelf life, but the pain we experience has no shelf life. So saying thank you for your service every time you see a person in uniform lifts the veil of hurt and offers the kindest thought of all.

The thought says, *I may not understand, but I respect you for your efforts and your sacrifices as you protect us and our country.* A thank you may lead to that serviceman or servicewoman finding peace and meaning with their past and truly understanding the freedoms we fight for.

I was resentful at the military for spraying me with Agent Orange. I was resentful at the military medical machine for sewing me up with cancer still present, and I resented how hard I thought life had become. Resentments can kill as war can. It's important to find the answers and to come to peace with resentments. I know that I was looking at what I didn't have or what was taken away. I was not looking at what I still had and that is much more than most.

I must move on.

Chapter Nineteen

LIVE EACH MOMENT

My family still gets together frequently. We like celebrations; we like happy times. We create occasions around birthdays, even six months early to surprise the birthday girls or boys, and around anniversaries, weddings, graduations, births—anything happy. Often, when these bashes occurred, we did not get 100 percent attendance. Not everyone was financially able to travel, especially if they had a family as most of us did. I wracked my brain on how we could sponsor a reunion and completely pay for it without having one or two of us shell out for it.

I Came Up with a Plan

With a strategic approach and the right timing, I decided I could get the family an invitation to be on the *Family Feud* TV game show, and of course, we would win the money. When we won, we'd put the proceeds toward a big family get-together. Note the adverb "when."

It took two years, two interviews, and two times the normal amount of patience to get on the show. I applied to have the family interviewed, first, in San Diego with the local station. The initial family members selected to be the on-screen participants were Mom and Dad and my youngest brother, David. They were selected because David worked for America West Airlines at the time and could fly himself and Mom and Dad into San Diego for free. I, being the instigator, was involved, and we had one slot left to fill. There apparently was a flipping of the coin back in the Midwest, and the oldest brother, Billy, won the toss and became the final contestant on our team. When we were assigned a date for the interview, we flew the team to San Diego for session number 1.

Billy, not known for being on time for scheduled events, raced out of his hotel room many minutes late. He always had to make just one more phone call, have one more drink, grab one more wink of sleep, or whatever. I, being my normal, calm self, threatened to push him out onto the street if we missed the interview.

Mom was in the back seat as the car raced down Route 163 toward Mission Valley. We headed for the Scottish Rite Temple—the location of the interviews. I forgot that Mom, due to her accidents, was a bit touchy about driving and not shy about telling me what I was doing wrong. In fact, after one accident, she wouldn't let the driver of any vehicle ever make a left turn. If we couldn't arrive at a preplanned destination with right turn after right turn, we couldn't go. But that day, I wasn't deterred, and my foot did not ease up on the accelerator. We took exit ramps at breakneck speeds, and I'm sure she would tell you "on two wheels," but that was not true. I ignored her intonations to the Lord to keep us safe, I ignored her driving instructions, and when asked, "Are you ignoring me?" I ignored that too. We raced into the auditorium and successfully passed the first level of interviews without a hitch.

Interview number 2 was conducted by a bigwig from Los Angeles who came to San Diego to question the finalists from America's Finest City. Calling him a bit pompous, understated his personality. We were dressed to the nines: suits, ties, and a nice dress for Mom who is calm as a cucumber since I didn't have to speed to the interview. I think she threatened to throw Billy out of the car herself if he wasn't on time. We sauntered into the Scottish Rite Temple confident and upbeat, and the dude from Los Angeles started in on us.

During the interview process in both cases, each person got questioned by the interviewer. I think the guy from Los Angeles was a director of the show, and he started out challenging Dad. He questioned every response rudely and acting like Dad failed the interview. He then started on Billy who was talking about his daughter, studying in Beijing. Billy used the correct pronunciation of the city's name, and the interviewer said, "Well, at least you said that correctly."

Then the bigwig set his sights on the youngest and most naive member of our team. I was holding my breath when he asked Davy what he did for a living. Davy proudly said, "I'm a customer service representative for America West Airlines." The interviewer said, "Don't you mean flight steward?" Undaunted or unaware of the dripping sarcasm, Davy said, "Oh no. One day we are on the plane, the next day we could be in baggage handling or acting as a ticketing agent. A new concept introduced by American West in the early 1980s."

Davy was our first sign of hope we might make it through this process. The next set of questions were aimed at me. I tapped patience I didn't know I had and strict military training and just said "Yes, sir" and "No, sir" and used silence to get out unscathed. I don't think I made a noticeable impression on him, but I also didn't tell him to pack it up any of his cavities, which was a major positive step for me. I had worked too hard for this opportunity, and I wasn't blowing it!

A-hole turned to Mom and transformed to sweetness and light. Of course, he was talking to a beautiful Catholic mother of ten and someone often described by the phrase "Well, sugar just wouldn't dare melt in her mouth." The director fell in love with Mom. He fawned all over her, and we got on the show. Sometimes it pays to keep your mouth shut and put Mom at the end of the line.

In September 1985, our big day came, and we headed to Los Angeles for the show's taping. We were all so excited and nervous. We had to go up the night before and stay in a hotel because we were scheduled to be in the studio at 7:00 a.m. The schedule includes the taping of five shows: one week's worth of *Family Feud* in one all-day session. We entered the studio at 7:00 a.m., and we didn't leave until about 7:00 p.m. Food was delivered for meals, and we sat all day in a sixty-five-degree environment, but we were so hyped up it didn't matter.

Our turn came, and we lined up, waiting for Richard Dawson to make his appearance. He sauntered in to loud applause and kissed Mom on the lips (ugh!). We were faced off against a family with three participants who were very, very old. We showed no mercy and won the first round, earning $666.

Next was the fast money round. We selected Dad and Billy to participate in that phase of the contest. We chose Billy because he was the fastest in our practice round in the hotel room before we came to the studio. This was serious stuff. We selected Dad because, oh, never mind. We needed two hundred points to win. Billy went first, racking up one hundred ninety points. Things don't happen randomly; there was a reason he won the coin toss. Dad brought it home, and we won a total of $10,666. Mine is not a story of *can't*.

Set Your Mind to It and Look What Happens

The show aired the day after Christmas 1985, and we all celebrated. Many of us held parties in our houses in different cities in the United States, inviting all our friends to share the moment. We all got on a conference call so we could hear the screaming nationwide. Instant celebrity status for the winners of *Family Feud* was garnered. We gave Billy the $666 to offset his flight costs, and we put the other $10,000 toward a one-week reunion in Cape Cod. We rented an eleven-room inn that boasted additional sleeping quarters in the barn, and we all fit—a snug fit but a fit nonetheless. We had 100 percent attendance, and it rained the entire week. I forgot to plan the weather. We still had a great time and reveled in the achievement and successes of the family.

* * *

I hosted our family reunion of 2014 at The Sofia Hotel in San Diego. The Sofia is a beautiful boutique hotel in the heart of the city. This towering brick structure was originally built in 1926 and named the Pickwick. After remodeling from the foundation to the roof in 2006, it reopened as the Sofia Hotel. She was the perfect hostess. We had forty-four immediate family members in attendance. People came from Wisconsin, Massachusetts, Ohio, South Carolina, Minnesota, Texas, California, Arizona, and parts unknown. Out-of-towners began arriving on Thursday evening, and the festivities began early Friday morning. There was golf at the famous Torrey Pines Golf Course, shopping, and general sightseeing during the day with a big kickoff Mexican buffet dinner aboard a Hornblower party boat in San Diego Bay. We were treated to a typically beautiful California sunset, fireworks, and excellent food.

At a hospitality suite in the Sofia, we congregated, drank, and caught up with one another until late in the evenings. Saturday saw another round of golf, at Balboa Park Golf Course this time, hiking at Torrey Pines State Reserve, a trip to the world-famous San Diego Zoo, and shopping.

At 6:00 p.m., we all met in the Currant American Brasserie, located in The Sofia, for a private reception with a mixologist who made special drinks named after us. At 7:00 p.m., eleven pedicabs pulled up in front of the restaurant to transport us to dinner. The bikes are sometimes covered, sometimes not, but they always have lights blazing and music blaring. I knew we would enjoy the six- or seven-block ride to our restaurant for that evening. What I didn't know was that the entire city of San Diego would enjoy it too.

We pulled out of the space in front of the restaurant, made a U-turn, and the eleven carriages roared down Broadway with lights blazing, music blaring, and the forty-four participants cheering, clapping, singing, and screaming. Traffic stopped, horns honked, people hung out car windows, cheering and clapping with us. Pedestrians stopped, waved, clapped, and yelled encouragement. It was a family moment, a community moment, and reminded me of what I missed from the sixties.

* * *

The significant moments continued. One day, I pushed my grocery cart through the radically crowded aisles of Costco, trying to reach the far end of the warehouse where the cases of toilet paper, paper towels, and water are located. I took the last turn on two wheels because I had so much to do. I came to a sudden and abrupt stop in a cart traffic jam. Everyone seemed to be studying ginormous cases of paper as if there was a crack-erjack prize in one of them. *People*, I thought, *they are all the same just grab one and get moving.* Eventually, I made my way to the pallets of water right behind a tiny, tiny woman. Her head barely looked over the handlebars of her shopping cart, and she was eyeing the cases of bottled water packed with thirty to forty bottles in a thin plastic casing. My thoughts were, "*Could you just sling that case on your cart and get moving. I'm very important, and you're impeding the progress of my life.*"

But I am not just my thoughts. I don't want to be that person. I have learned that I am more than my thoughts and, in many cases like this, better than my thoughts. I act the person I want to be with heart, soul, and caring for others.

I believe I choose my thoughts, my perceptions, and my actions. None of those are by accident, by fate, or caused by others.

I abandoned my cart, walked up to the woman, and asked her permission to put a case on her cart for her. She was not surprised. She acted as if she were waiting for me to do just that. She immediately responded, "Yes, please. Put it on the bottom shelf of the cart if you don't mind." She came from a culture of love and respect, she came from a culture that respected age and differences, she was Vietnamese. She accepted the offer of help as the norm, not as a reflection of her age, her frailty or her size. People in community, not people fighting for position or material items. A community based on love, respect, and strength shared on an intimate level.

I always thought of intimacy as between lovers, but words synonymous with intimacy are closeness, togetherness, affinity, and rapport. When I lifted the water for the stranger, who benefited most? I can't know for certain, but I felt you couldn't measure the difference between us because we both left the encounter with more. More strength, more love, more support, and more affinity. It wasn't that I gave, and she took. It wasn't that I used my power over her. She gave as much back in respect, gratitude, and admiration.

In addition, the lady behind me watched the transaction and said, "Oh my, that was so sweet, so nice." She benefited as well. As I moved up in the queue to pick up my case of water, I looked at that same lady behind me as I struggled to get my own case of water in the cart. Jokingly, I said, "Now, if I could just get someone to help me with my water."

She laughed and said, "I should have helped you and paid it forward."

There was no doubt she could have helped me. We were equals laughing, sharing, joking, and making the experience lighter and more enjoyable, and we were strangers.

When I stopped thinking about myself and engaged in acts of kindness, I found strength and hope. It helped me build the resolve to go on and live in this society and feel some purpose.

I think of it as a bank account. I'm not hurting right this minute, but if pain is just around the corner, I want to have some love and hope in the account to draw from. It's all about balance. It's not about forgetting or remembering or trudging on. Yesterday is a memory, and tomorrow is hopes and dreams; all I have is today. What I do today builds new memories for my history. And today I want a history I can be proud of—a history that reflects who I truly am.

I am not my story. I am not the victim of my story. My story is just a retelling of events on my journey. The events of the past do not and will not predict my future. It's impossible to continue thinking this might happen again because I attracted it, caused it, or wanted it. In many cases, the events were not even about me; they were about someone else or something else.

When I lived in the silence, seclusion, and the darkness of the past, I created nothing new, and I had nothing left to live for because I became my thoughts. I became my story. I needed love, strength, and courage to go on, and I needed the intimacy of human interactions, whether I thought I was worthy of it or not, whether I wanted it or not. The missing link was I had to *create* it. It wasn't going to just fly in the window and land in my lap.

I had not wanted to go on. Was it a rebellious act because I wasn't accepted? Was it my reaction to not feeling loved? Was it the personal disappointment of failure? Or was it just exhaustion because I had to fight so hard to survive and fight so long just to be me? I saw, heard, and felt the roadblocks placed my path that prevented me from moving forward as myself. I saw the hurdles I had to clear, and as I jumped them, I got tired. There always are hurdles. I saw how hard it was for women in the 1960s, and I saw people of color in the 1970s struggle just to survive, and I wondered why? I was gay in the 1980s when many were dying of AIDS. Life can be difficult. I didn't want my history to read that I made it worse by limiting other's role, making them take lunch on the back porch or marry only people of the opposite sex.

I am the only one that can create love and romance in my life and make it part of my history.

And I have.

* * *

I'm a romantic at heart. When my spouse left to travel out of town for work, I'd sneak a card in his suitcase that said I love you and miss you. When he arrived at his destination and unpacked in a hotel room and found the card, he knew he was not alone. When I had to leave on a trip, I'd leave cards all over the house. In the refrigerator and in the cupboard next to the cereal. When sleepy-eyed spouse reached for the milk, "I love you" awaited him.

One Christmas, my spouse wanted a ring—an expensive ring. I initially said, "This year hasn't been great financially, so we can't afford something that extravagant. Let's be conservative this holiday season." Begrudgingly, he agreed. I bought the ring anyway and wanted to create a romantic surprise. No, it wasn't in a cake like I did for Doris. That year we had a gold-and-white Christmas color scheme in all the decorations, so I wrapped the ring box in white paper with gold ribbon. Then I thought how recognizable that looked. Anyone would be able to guess it was a ring. So I purchased a sheet of Styrofoam and cut twenty-three cubes the size of a ring box and wrapped all of them in white paper with gold ribbon. I then hung the twenty-four white and gold boxes on the tree like ornaments. We opened all our presents, and when the other half thought we were done, I said, "There's one more, and you have to find it." Half the fun was watching him tear open the tree decorations until he found his ring.

Romantic

When I accept others as they are, I share the love, the power, and the strength created with each of them. That strength replenishes some of those attributes that have been depleted by the daily grind and, in some cases, by tragedy and trauma. I can use these gifts when the road gets a little tough. I see them as gifts, and they give me the courage and the awareness that I can go on with the help and support of others on a much deeper and more meaningful level. I can go on to share these gifts if I don't go silent, and I don't go within to become that story.

We are only as sick as our secrets.

Chapter Twenty

DESIGN OF LIFE

This is a story about life, and I happen to be in it. I am not the seven-year-old failure reflected in my father's eyes, and maybe I'm not the son Dad wanted, but I was the perfect son for him. It wasn't about me. He needed to grow and expand his horizons, and I was just the vehicle that gave him that opportunity. I didn't get to pick and choose my experiences in many cases, and I certainly didn't get to pick and choose my parents, my children, or my pain, but I do get to choose how I deal with life experiences. I choose my perceptions of life, my thoughts, my actions, and create my beliefs. My beliefs are evolving day by day, and so is my life.

* * *

William Blake said, "The experienced life is far more fulfilling than the blissful and innocent life." I lost my innocence, and I don't want it back. It's been replaced with experience that gave me strength and wisdom beyond my expectations, and most importantly, a sense of peace that is the foundation on which I can face difficult circumstances.

I always felt I wasn't enough. I wasn't strong enough, fast enough, smart enough, or handsome enough to be okay in this world because I was looking outside me for the strength and will to carry on. The person I thought I was supposed to be eluded me. I wasn't aware that I always was the person I was meant to be. I didn't learn in school that I should put on my jacket and go next door for help. Flight school didn't teach me to get in touch with and listen to my intuitive thoughts. I wasn't informed by anyone that the heart has as much to say as the brain. I did not have a role model who said it's okay to feel safe and at home in the arms of a man.

I believe I was born with everything I need to survive. My problem was I wasn't in touch with that concept and aware of all that I had. I kept looking for the "missing link" to me. Was I not in line when courage was passed out? Was I napping when strength was administered? What's missing? Oh, poor me! Others got the looks, the nice small firm butt, the brains, and the brawn.

* * *

When adversity hits, I can take the path labeled "victim," or I can march on with the awareness and knowledge created by experience. Strength and hope will become part of the fabric of me and be of service to others. What I experience, learn, and live to tell about is not failure, not heartache and loss, not bad luck but a decidedly purposeful event in the development of who I am today and who I will become tomorrow.

There are no accidents in life. I think of entitlement as "I deserve." But more importantly, why did I think I was entitled to a life without challenges, without struggle, and without hurt? The black holes of my past are not predictors of what will happen to me in the future; they are honed weapons and tools I will use to weather new storms. I answered the question, "Will I be okay in the face of new adversity?" with a resounding "yes" because I've been made strong. I found the strength within, and I have a foundation of confidence that I will share with others to help them weather storms.

When I asked, "Why me?" the answer was, "Why not you?" Should these negative, unfortunate, and horrible events happen to someone else? What I have experienced has made me the person I am today, and I'm proud of that person. I'm probably not the brightest stripe on the flag, I'm probably not going to be asked to the prom anytime soon, but there is no better me. The good news is if I keep up this outlook and belief, I get stronger. More importantly, I have hope. Hope is not a glistening vision of a golden future; it's the absence of fear.

Hope does not include the possibility that I'll get to design my life. If I could, I'd like to be six feet tall, with wavy blond hair that always looks good, slightly tanned skin, deep blue eyes that make people melt, tons of money, and four hundred thousand likes for every social media post. And of course, a dedicated staff to attend to my every need and to handle all life problems for me. Oh yeah, and a relationship with a life partner that is simple, easy, and loving. I could go on and on. Now that's blissful and ignorant thinking. Did Blake say innocent?

Just for the record, I didn't get that. What I really needed was a design for living. I do not believe in a malevolent force of nature or a God who said, "Okay, let's put this guy in a prim and proper New England Irish Catholic family. Let's give him a macho and tough father, then let's throw him from the car, send him to war, remove the left side of his face, and have him marry and father three children only to find out he's gay." That would be one mean force and mean to more than just me. Life is life. I'm just a bit player trying to do his part.

When I was sitting behind that dune my first night in Nam, I wish I could have said, "This is not about me." But the rockets distracted me, the fear consumed me, and the outcome appalled me. So do I wallow in that moment, do I let the sounds, the sights, and the feelings consume me, or do I move on?

In my case, the experiences were so altering that I couldn't see, feel, or find me, so I had to start over and create a new me. With no way forward and no way back, I had to start from scratch and rebuild. The new me isn't consumed by a single event, thought, or feeling. I can be very, very sad that my brother passed away, and yet flying to his funeral, I can enjoy and laugh with my daughter as she's about to get us jailed as terrorists.

I don't get to dictate the terms of my life; I didn't get to sign a prenuptial in case things went wrong in my life. I do get to live life on life's terms. That force or power of life is not malevolent, sadistic, or sarcastic although if there is such a thing, it's a force that is laughing while I'm making other plans for my life. I believe I was born with everything I needed to be successful. I have all the power, strength, courage, love, and hope that I need to succeed. It's within me and always has been. My job is to become aware of those assets and hone them throughout the years. Hone them so I can unlock that power from within, set it in motion to protect me and keep me strong and safe no matter what. I have that today. No matter what.

Maybe why what happened to me didn't happen to someone else is because I could handle it, and they couldn't. They get a different set of circumstances to deal with because that's what they can manage. They become experienced in a different way with different tools. That might be the definition of divine balance.

The benefits of tough experiences are not realized instantaneously, but there are benefits and rewards for trudging on.

Marianne Williamson's poem "Our Deepest Fear" contradicted my thoughts about not being enough. She said, "Our deepest fear is not that we are inadequate. / Our deepest fear is that we are powerful beyond measure. / It's our light not our darkness that frightens us.... / Your playing small does not serve the world. / There's nothing enlightened about shrinking so other people won't feel insecure around you. We are all meant to shine. / And as we let our own light shine, / We unconsciously give other people permission to do the same. / As we're liberated from our own fear, / Our presence automatically liberates others."

When I shine, I give those around me permission to shine as well. Maybe I can put light and hope on a dark moment and give new perspective to the events and circumstances surrounding another in a challenging and tough world.

I can have mind-blowing experiences, I can have a broken heart, and I can feel rejected and unloved, abused, and neglected. In response, I can just lie down and die or go within to find the resolve to go on. I would not be who I am if I didn't experience everything that happened to me exactly as it happened to me.

In fact, I'm quite sure I'd be a different person, and I'm not sure I'd like that person because I'm proud of me, I'm happy with the person I've become, and I want to share that journey.

That's my spirituality. I used to think spirituality was a monk on a mountaintop contemplating his navel; that's not me. When I'm on the mountaintop, I contemplate someone else's navel. I think there are many forms of spirituality. Those so inclined to sit on a ledge may end up writing books that aid millions or creating a movement that engulfs throngs of people and helps move them on up the plane of life to a higher purpose. But that's not me. I think living a spiritual life means being the best me I can possibly be. It means not hiding, not keeping secrets, not judging me or others but to shine as the best me I can possibly be. If I shine from the depth of my soul, others too can shine, and *we* change the moments one at a time.

* * *

Dad, you didn't ask, and you didn't tell, and the reasons are your own. You created me, and you didn't approve or accept. You didn't need to approve. You just needed to accept me and love me as I am and be as proud of me as I am proud to be the son who changed your life and your perceptions of the world.

We came from "don't ask, don't tell" to discussing the coming out process at my Father's eulogy held in a Catholic Church. Lightning didn't strike, the walls of the church are still intact, and the family continues to grow—grows to accept gay cousins and a lesbian granddaughter who, at fifteen, said, "Will you stop asking me if I'm a lesbian? You already know I am." We came from the day before I died to a day we can live with pride, love, and acceptance.

The brain is not the most important tool in decision-making and surviving life's challenges. I do know my brain wants to take over and run the show. My brain cancels out my feeling and intuitions and says logic wins the day. I know today I am much more powerful than my brain. My brain is like an egotistical child who wants his way and his toys and his life. The expression about becoming a man and giving up childish ways and childish things is apropos. I thought that was about my tricycle and my tops and my wagon. Maybe it is about how I viewed and thought about life and my role in it—about how I made decisions and how I loved and how I behaved as I walked the path of my life. I'm not a victim of my life, my parentage, or my war. I'm privileged to have played a role, to have influenced, to have loved, and to have had an impact in this world however small. Today I have achieved balance between the outside and the inside. I am the man I'm supposed to be, and I see it, feel it, and in most cases, live it.

Peace comes from within. Today nothing has changed about the past, and everything about the future is bright and full of hope because I am loved, and I'm strong again.

I have a life worth living because I chose to live.

Epilogue

The quiet of explosive doom
The darkness of shrouded panic
The fear of tomorrow
Believed immutable has passed

Silence has become the spirit of hope
Darkness will usher in the comfort of rest
Fear stands as the protector, not the foe

Life grows ever larger
The sun shines ever brighter
Laughter rings loud
Because I lived

CPSIA information can be obtained
at www.ICGtesting.com
Printed in the USA
LVHW111504240221
679840LV00013B/356

9 781645 449133